My Ten Years
in a Quandary
AND HOW THEY GREW

My Ten Years
in a
Quandary

AND HOW THEY GREW

by

ROBERT BENCHLEY

ÆONIAN PRESS

Leyden, Mass. 01337

Republished 1976 by Special Arrangement
with Harper and Row Publishers, Inc.

Copyright © 1936 by Robert C. Benchley

Library of Congress Cataloging in Publication Data

Benchley, Robert Charles, 1889-1945.
  My ten years in a quandary and how they grew.

  Reprint of the 1940 ed. published by Blue Ribbon Books.
New York.
  I. Title.
PS3503.E49M9   1976   818'.5'207   76-6516
ISBN 0-88411-303-5

AEONIAN PRESS, INC.
Box 476
Jackson Heights, New York 11372

*Manufactured in the United States of America
by Inter-Collegiate Press, Inc. Mission, Kansas*

Table of Contents

vi

My Ten Years
in a Quandary
AND HOW THEY GREW

The
Lost Locomotive

THE day that Mr. MacGregor lost the locomotive was a confusing one for our accountants. They didn't know whom to charge it to.

"We have an account here called 'Alterations,'" said the head accountant (Mr. MacGregor). "We might charge it to that. Losing a locomotive is certainly an alteration in something."

"I am afraid that you are whistling in the dark, Mr. MacGregor," I said quietly.

"The point is not what account we are going to charge the lost locomotive to," I continued. "It is how you happened to lose it."

"I have already told you," he replied, with a touch of asperity, "that I haven't the slightest idea. I was tired and nervous and—well—I lost it, that's all!

"As a matter of fact," he snapped, "I am not at all sure that the locomotive is lost. And, if it is, I am not at all sure that I lost it."

*   *   *   *   *

"I don't think that we need go into that point," I replied. "When a man takes a locomotive out and comes back without it, and is unable to explain what has become of it, the presumption is that he, personally, has lost it. How did you like those tangerines we had for lunch?"

"Only fair," MacGregor answered.

"You see?" I said. "You are getting cynical."

We have had a great deal of trouble about Mr. MacGregor's growing cynical. He looks at things with a bilious eye. It is bringing down the morale of the office force, and there are whole days at a time when we don't sell a thing.

*   *   *   *   *

"How often do you take that medicine I gave you?" I asked him.

MacGregor winced slightly. "Hot-diggidy!" he replied.

"That is not an answer to my question," I said, sternly.

"What were we just talking about?" he asked.

"You mean the tangerines?" I said, his cynicism still rankling in my mind.

"No," he replied. "Before that."

2

We both thought for a minute.

"Well, it couldn't have been very important," I said, laughing. This got him in good humor and we swung forward, double-time, along the road to work.

"Take the Witness!"

NEWSPAPER accounts of trial cross-examinations always bring out the cleverest in me. They induce day dreams in which I am the witness on the stand, and if you don't know some of my imaginary comebacks to an imaginary cross-examiner (Doe vs. Benchley: 482-U.S.-367-398), you have missed some of the most stimulating reading in the history of American jurisprudence.

These little reveries usually take place shortly after I have read the transcript of a trial, while I am on a long taxi ride or seated at a desk with plenty of other work to to. I like them best when I have work to to, as they deplete me mentally so that I am forced to go and lie down after a particularly sharp verbal rally. The knowledge that I have completely floored my adversary, and the imaginary congratulations of my friends (also imaginary), seem more worth while than any amount of fiddling work done.

During these cross-questionings I am always

4

*I just sit there, burning him up with
each answer*

very calm. Calm in a nice way, that is—never
cocky. However frantic my inquisitor may wax
(and you should see his face at times—it's pur-
ple!), I just sit there, burning him up with
each answer, winning the admiration of the
courtroom, and, at times, even a smile from the
judge himself. At the end of my examination
the judge is crazy about me.

Just what the trial is about, I never get quite
clear in my mind. Sometimes the subject
changes in the middle of the questioning, to
allow for the insertion of an especially good
crack on my part. I don't think that I am ever

actually the defendant, although I don't know why I should feel that I am immune from trial by a jury of my peers—if such exist.

I am usually testifying in behalf of a friend, or perhaps as just an impersonal witness for someone whom I do not know, who, naturally, later becomes my friend for life. It is Justice that I am after—Justice and a few well-spotted laughs.

Let us whip right into the middle of my cross-examination, as I naturally wouldn't want to pull my stuff until I had been insulted by the lawyer, and you can't really get insulted simply by having your name and address asked. I am absolutely fair about these things. If the lawyer will treat me right, I'll treat him right. He has got to start it. For a decent cross-examiner, there is no more tractable witness in the world than I am.

Advancing toward me, with a sneer on his face, he points a finger at me. (I have sometimes thought of pointing my finger back at him, but have discarded that as being too fresh. I don't have to resort to clowning.)

* * * * *

Q—You think you're pretty funny, don't you?
(*I have evidently just made some mildly hu-*

morous comeback, nothing smart-alecky, but good enough to make him look silly.)

A—I have never given the matter much thought.

Q—Oh, you haven't given the matter much thought, eh? Well, you seem to be treating this examination as if it were a minstrel show.

A *(very quietly and nicely)*—I have merely been taking my cue from your questions. *(You will notice that all this presupposes quite a barrage of silly questions on his part, and pat answers on mine, omitted here because I haven't thought them up. At any rate, it is evident that I have already got him on the run before this reverie begins.)*

Q—Perhaps you would rather that I conducted this inquiry in baby talk?

A—If it will make it any easier for you. *(Pandemonium, which the Court feels that it has to quell, although enjoying it obviously as much as the spectators.)*

Q *(furious)*—I see. Well, here is a question that I think will be simple enough to elicit an honest answer: Just how did you happen to know that it was eleven-fifteen when you saw the defendant?

A—Because I looked at my watch.

7

Q—And just why did you look at your watch at this particular time?

A—To see what time it was.

Q—Are you accustomed to looking at your watch often?

A—That is one of the uses to which I often put my watch.

Q—I see. Now, it couldn't, by any chance, have been ten-fifteen instead of eleven-fifteen when you looked at your watch this time, could it?

A—Yes, sir. It could.

Q—Oh, it *could* have been ten-fifteen?

A—Yes, sir—if I had been in Chicago. *(Not very good, really. I'll work up something better. I move to have that answer stricken from the record.)*

*   *   *   *   *

When I feel myself lowering my standards by answering like that, I usually give myself a rest, and, unless something else awfully good pops into my head, I adjourn the court until next day. I can always convene it again when I hit my stride.

If possible, however, I like to drag it out until I have really given my antagonist a big final wallop which practically curls him up on the floor (I may think of one before this goes to

8

press), and, wiping his forehead, he mutters, "Take the witness!"

As I step down from the stand, fresh as a daisy, there is a round of applause which the Court makes no attempt to silence. In fact, I have known certain judges to wink pleasantly at me as I take my seat. Judges are only human, after all.

My only fear is that, if I ever really am called upon to testify in court, I won't be asked the right questions. That *would* be a pretty kettle of fish!

The New Strokes

I T WILL be interesting to see what the new season will bring out in the way of novel swimming strokes. I'll bet it involves the use of an auxiliary motor strapped on the shoulders.

When I was learning to swim, people just swam. The idea was to keep afloat and, in an orderly fashion, to get somewhere if possible. If there was nowhere you wanted to get to, you just swam quietly 'round and 'round until your lips got blue. Then you went in.

The stroke that I was first taught was known as the "breast, or gondola, stroke." High out of the water by the bows. It was dignified and stately and went something like this: "One-two-three-sink! One-two-three-sink!" The legs were shot out straight behind, like a frog's, except that they were not good to eat.

*   *   *   *   *

Then the more sporting among the swimming crowd took to swimming tipped over on one side, with one ear dragging in the water.

You just swam quietly 'round
and 'round

This was considered very athletic, especially if one arm was lifted out of the water at each stroke. But even then the procedure was easy-going, pleasant, and more of a pastime than a chore. It was considered very bad form to churn.

But with the advent of the various "crawls," swimming took on more the nature of a battle with the elements. You had to lash at the water, tear at the waves with your teeth, snort and spit, kick your feet like a child with tantrums and, in general, behave as if you had set out deliberately to drown yourself in an epilepsy. It became tiring just to watch.

*   *   *   *   *

I never learned the names of the new strokes

as they came along, but I gather that the instructions for some of them must read:

The Australian Wrench: Place the head under water up to the shoulder blades. Bring the left arm up, over and around the neck until the fingers of the left hand touch the right cheek (still under water). Shove the right arm sideways and to the left until the right shoulder touches the chin. Then shift arm positions suddenly, and with great splashing, propelling the body through the water by lashing upward and downward with the feet and legs. The head is kept under water during the entire race, thereby eliminating both wind-resistance and breathing. It is bully fun.

The Navajo Twist: Rotate the entire body like a bobbin on the surface of the water, with elbows and knees bent. Spit while the mouth is on the up-side. Inhale when it is under. This doesn't get you much of anywhere, but it irritates the other swimmers and makes it difficult for them to swim.

The Lighthouse Churn: Just stand still, in water about up to your waist, and beat at the surface with your fists, snorting and spitting at the same time. This does nothing but make you conspicuous, but, after all, what is modern swimming for?

Contributors to This Issue

UNFORTUNATELY the current issue of our magazine has had to be abandoned because of low visibility and an epidemic of printers' nausea, but we felt that our readers would still want to know a little something of the private lives of our contributors. At any rate, here we go:

ELWOOD M. CRINGE, who contributed the article *Is Europe?* is a graduate of Moffard College and, since graduation, has specialized in high tension rope. He is thirty-two years old, wears a collar, and his hobbies are golf, bobbing for apples, and junket.

HAL GARMISCH, author of *How It Feels to Be Underslung*, writes: "I am young, good-looking and would like to meet a girl about my own age who likes to run. I have no hobbies, but I am crazy about kitties."

MEDFORD LAZENBY probably knows more about people, as such, than anyone in the country, unless it is people themselves. He has been all over the world in a balloon-rigged ketch and has a fascinating story to tell. *China Through a Strainer,* in this issue, is not it.

*   *   *   *   *

ELIZABETH FEDELLER, after graduation from Ruby College for Near-Sighted Girls, had a good time for herself among the deserted towns of Montana and writes of her experiences in a style which has been compared unfavorably with that of Ernest Hemingway. She is rather unattractive looking.

On our request for information, GIRLIE TENNAFLY wrote us that he is unable to furnish any, owing to a short memory. He contributed the article on *Flanges: Open and Shut,* which is not appearing in this issue.

We will let ESTHER RUBRIC tell about herself: "Strange as it may seem," writes Miss Rubric, "I am not a 'high-brow,' although I write on what are known as 'high-brow' subjects. I am really quite a good sport, and love to play tennis (or 'play at' tennis, as I call it), and am always ready for a good romp. My mother and father were missionaries in Boston, and I was brought up in a strictly family way. We children used to be thought strange by all the other 'kids' in Boston because my brothers had beards and I fell down a lot. But, as far as

I can see, we all grew up to be respectable citizens, in a pig's eye. When your magazine accepted my article on *How to Decorate a Mergenthaler Linotype Machine,* I was in the 'seventh heaven.' I copied it, word for word, from Kipling."

* * * * *

DARG GAMM is too well known to our readers to call for an introduction. He is now at work on his next-but-one novel and is in hiding with the Class óf 1915 of Zanzer College, who are preparing for their twentieth reunion in June.

We couldn't get IRVIN S. COBB or CLARENCE BUDINGTON KELLAND to answer our request for manuscripts.

Dog
Libel

A FRIEND of mine who calls himself a dachshund is furious over an article he has just read in a scientific paper purporting to give the essential qualities of a good dachshund. He finds himself libelled by implication.

"I think I could sue," said my friend. "This man here has said, in effect, that I am not a real dachshund."

"I wouldn't sue," I advised, cautiously. "In the first place, you would have to show that you had been damaged by the publication of the article. Your standing in this household is just the same as it was before the article was written. We won't go into just what your standing *is*, but it remains unchanged at any rate.

"Furthermore," I added, sagely, "the magazine, pushed to the wall, might dig up a lot of ugly stories which you might not relish having told in court. You are not immaculate, you know. Remember that Seelyham named 'Arthur.'"

"That was just wrestling in fun," my friend said. "I meant him no harm."

* * * * *

"Just the same," I warned, "it wouldn't look very well in the tabloids. And, anyway, the case wouldn't come up for a year or so, and even then it would drag on, with appeals and re-appeals, until you were flat broke. I couldn't do very much to help you out with the costs, you know."

This rather sobered him up, I thought. He had evidently been more or less counting on me to back him in this crack-brained suit of his.

"Listen to this!" he said, trying to swing me into his own irrational state of mind. He spread the paper out on the floor with his paw and adjusted his spectacles. (He wears them only for very fine print.)

I am afraid that this account is getting to sound just a mite whimsical, what with dogs wearing spectacles and talking like people. My only excuse is that it is an actual stenographic account of a conversation and is designed only to show the futility of libel suits.

* * * * *

"Listen to this," he said (we will leave out

the spectacles this time) : " 'The special work of a dachshund is to enter a badger hole and hold the attention of the animal until it can be dug out.'

"I never saw a badger," he said, without looking up from the paper, "much less try to hold its attention. How do you hold a badger's attention, anyway?"

"I shouldn't think that it would be very hard," I said. "You could make faces, or just say 'Look, badger!' I don't imagine that a badger's mind wanders easily, once the badger has caught sight of something."

"That is beside the point, anyway," he said, crossly. "The point is that I do not go into badger-holes myself. Does that, or does it not, imply that I am not a real dachshund?"

"You are too touchy," I said. "There must be plenty of real dachshunds in this country who don't go near a badger-hole from one year's end to the other. No jury in the world would count that as a personal slur on you."

*　　*　　*　　*　　*

"Very well, then—here is another crack: 'The hind legs should be strong and capable, and viewed from behind must go down straight and by no means show the turning in at the heel

18

known as cow-hocks. This is very common and very bad.' Why doesn't he mention my name and be done with it? Why doesn't he come right out and say Friedel Immerman is not a genuine dachhund?"

"Could you prove in a court of law that you *are* a genuine dachshund?" I asked, trying not to be brutal about it.

He turned in disgust and walked away without deigning a reply. As he disappeared through the door I distinctly saw the "turning in at the heel known as cow-hocks. Very common and very bad."

It probably is just as well that he dropped the suit.

The Rope Trick
Explained

IN EXPLAINING this trick, I need hardly say that it is known as "the Indian rope trick." That is the only trick that everyone explains, as well as the only trick that no one has ever seen. (Now don't write in and say that you have a friend who has seen it. I know your friend and he drinks.)

For readers under the age of three (of whom, judging from several letters at hand, I have several) I will explain that "the Indian rope trick" consists in throwing a rope into the air, where it remains, apparently unfastened to anything, while a boy climbs up to the top. Don't ask me what he does then.

This trick is very easy to explain. The point is that the boy gets up into the air somehow and *drops the rope down to the ground*, makit look as if the reverse were true. This is only one way to do it, however. There are millions of ways.

*　　*　　*　　*　　*

While in India, a friend of mine, a Mr. Mac-Gregor, assisted me in confusing the natives, in more ways than one. We dressed up in Indian costume, for one thing. This confused even us, but we took it good-naturedly.

Then I announced to a group of natives, who were standing open-mouthed (ready to bite us, possibly) that Mr. MacGregor and I would perform the famous Indian Rope Trick under their very noses. This was like stealing thunder from a child.

Stationing myself at the foot of a rope which extended upward into the air with no apparent support at the other end, I suggested to Mr. MacGregor that he climb it.

"Who—me?" he asked, hitching his tunic around his torso.

This took up some time, during which part of our audience left. The remainder were frankly incredulous, as was Mr. MacGregor. I, however, stuck to my guns.

"Up you go, MacGregor!" I said. "You used to be in the Navy!"

*　*　*　*　*

So, like a true yeoman, Mr. MacGregor laid hands on the rope and, in a trice, was at its top. It wasn't a very good trice, especially when viewed from below, but it served to bring a gasp of astonishment from the little group, many of whom walked away.

"Come on in—the water's fine!" called Mr. MacGregor, waving from his pinnacle (one waves from one's pinnacle sideways in India).

"Is everything fast?" I called up at him.

"Everything fast and burning brightly, sir!" answered Mr. MacGregor, like a good sailor.

"Then—*let 'er go!*" I commanded, sounding *Taps* on a little horn I had just found in my hand.

And, *mirabile dictu,* Mr. MacGregor disappeared into thin air and *drew the rope up after him!* Even I had to look twice. It was a stupendous victory for the occult.

*   *   *   *   *

"Are there any questions?" I asked the mob.

"What is Clark Gable like?" someone said.

"He's a very nice fellow," I answered. "Modest and unassuming. I see quite a lot of him when I am in Hollywood."

There was a scramble for my autograph at this, and the party moved on, insisting that I go with them for a drink and tell them more about their favorite movie stars. There is a native drink in India called *"straite-ri"* which is very cooling.

* * * * *

It wasn't until I got back to our New York office that I saw Mr. MacGregor again, and I forgot to ask him how he ever got down.

Toddling
Along

WHAT is the disease which manifests itself in an inability to leave a party—any party at all—until it is all over and the lights are being put out? It must be some form of pernicious inertia.

No matter where I am, if there are more than four people assembled in party formation, I must always be the last to leave. I may not be having a very good time; in fact, I may wish that I had never come at all. But I can't seem to bring myself to say, "Well, I guess I'll be toddling along."

Other people are able to guess they'll be toddling along. One by one, and two by two, and sometimes in great groups, I watch them toddle along, until I am left, with possibly just my host to keep me company. Sometimes even my host asks me if I mind if *he* toddles along to bed. When this happens, I am pretty quick to take the hint.

I have often thought of hiring a little man to go about with me, just to say to my host:

Sometimes even my host asks me if I mind if he toddles along to bed

"Well, old Bob thinks he'll be toddling along now." It's that initial plunge that I can't seem to negotiate. It isn't that I *can't* toddle. It's that I can't *guess* I'll toddle.

*   *   *   *   *

I suppose that part of this mania for staying is due to a fear that, if I go, something good will happen and I'll miss it. Somebody might do card tricks, or shoot somebody else. But this doesn't account for it all. It is much deeper seated than that.

The obvious explanation to an analyst would

be that I have an aversion to going *home*, because I have a sister fixation or am subconsciously in love with my parrot and am seeking an escape.

This, as I am so fond of saying to analysts, is not true. I would much rather be at home than at most parties. In fact, I don't go to many parties, and for that very reason.

My diagnosis would be that it is a sign of a general break-up. I have difficulty in starting to do anything, but once started, I can't stop. I find myself at a party and I have to stay at a party until I am put out.

The next step is, I am afraid, that I won't be able to find myself at all.

Oh, well.

No Pullmans, Please!

I SUPPOSE that it is just looking for trouble on my part, but what are they going to do with all the old Pullman cars when the streamliners come into general use? I hope that they don't try to palm one of them off on me.

I simply couldn't take care of an old Pullman. I haven't got the space, in the first place. It's all I can do to find room for my big bag after I have unpacked it. Imagine trying to crowd a pullman in, too!

Neither have I the inclination. I see no reason why I should be made to take over something that I really don't want, do you? And yet I have a horrible premonition that some day soon they are going to drag around a car named "Gleeber's Falls" or "Angostura" and ask me to give it a home.

*   *   *   *   *

The first time I read about the advent of the new type of sleeping car, I said, quick as a flash: "Here it comes! I get the old ones!"

They've got to do *some*thing with all those "Laburnums" and "Latvias." And I always seem to get things like that. "Give it to old Bob," people say, when they are tearing down their houses. "It will be just right for his room!"

I am to blame, in a way, for a long time ago I set out to furnish a room in a sort of knick-knack fashion. I even invited contributions from my friends. But what I meant was contributions that I could use. I didn't mean that I was starting a whaling museum or that I planned to build more rooms. I had more or less in mind a mid-Victorian study of the "what-not" variety. Well, I got my "what-nots."

* * * * *

It began with little articles to line up on top of a bookcase, miniature geese, little men with baskets, shells with eggs in them and broken stags. I also was not averse to hanging oddments on the walls. My friends entered into the spirit of this admirably. Every one had fun but the lady who dusted.

Then people began looking around town for heavier gifts. It got to be a game. Trucks began arriving with old busts of Sir Walter Scott, four-foot statues of men whose shirtfronts lit up when attached to an electric connection, stuffed owls and fox terriers that had lain too long at the taxidermist's. This phase ended with the gift of a small two-headed calf in a moderate state of preservation.

From then on the slogan became: "Send it to Benchley!" Wrecking concerns were pressed into service, and chipped cornices from the old Post Office, detached flights of stairs, hitching posts and railings began pouring in. Every day was like Christmas in Pompeii. The overflow went into the bedroom and I started sleeping under an old spinet, covered over with a set of bead-curtains which had been brought to me from a bordello in Marseille.

* * * * *

The friendly mood in which the game started changed gradually to one of persecution. The idea began to embarrass me and to make it impossible for me to move about. On several occasions it became a matter for the police, and once the Missing Persons Bureau took a hand in it and searched my room for a runaway college girl. They found nothing, however, but three Chinese laborers who had been smuggled into the country and delivered to my place in a caterer's wagon.

So perhaps I have a right to be worried about

It got to be a game

those out-of-date Pullmans. I have had stranger things foisted on me. I think that this time I will put my foot down. At the first sign of a Pullman being brought up the stairs I will bolt the door, leaving my friends to their own devices with it. I don't want any more truck in this room, much less a full-blown Pullman, and, ungracious as it may seem, I don't intend to have it.

Mysteries
from the Sky

I THINK that I am violating no confidence when I say that Nature holds many mysteries which we humans have not fathomed as yet. Some of them may not even be worth fathoming.

What, for instance, do we know of the many strange things which fall from the sky? I don't mean old overshoes and snaffle-bits, which everybody knows about, but those large masses of nergium and philutium which are always dropping out of nowhere onto Kansas and Oklahoma.

They have never been actually identified as nergium and philutium, because I made those names up, but they certainly are some form of calci-colocate $(Cb_2Ci_2M_3)$ or Sneeden's Disease. When subjected to a white heat this substance explodes with a loud bang (Ba_2Ng_2) and is never seen or heard of again. And see if I care!

*   *   *   *   *

The most famous deposit of this kind occurred near Dormant, Kansas, in 1846. Following a heavy thunderstorm during the night
workers in the fields were more surprised than
pleased to find that a whole new State had been
added to the Union right on top of their wheat,
apparently having dropped from the sky. This
made it necessary to elect two more Senators
to go to Congress and to have one more State
fair each year. All this resulted in the Civil
War.

The so-called "rain of frogs" in North Da-
kota in 1859 was another mix-up. Enoch Kaffer,
a farmer, was walking along the road near Oy-
ster Bed one day when he was hit on the head
by a falling frog. On looking up to see where
it had come from, he was hit over the eye with
another frog. Deciding that it was time to get
out of there, he started to run, but soon found
himself pelted on all sides by a rain of frogs,
all in an ugly humor.

On reaching home Kaffer told his experience
to his wife, who divorced him. That she had a
certain amount of right on her side was shown
by subsequent investigations which disclosed no
sign of any frogs or even frog footprints in the
neighborhood of where he had been. Kaffer

himself, however, stoutly maintained his innocence and finally went insane.

* * * * *

Another somewhat similar case is recorded in what was then Indian Territory. An Indian by the name of Ferguson was missing from his home for two days, and on finally returning said that he had been delayed by being hit by a falling meteorite which had come flaming through the sky at him as he was crossing a field.

As proof of his story he displayed an ugly cut across the bridge of his nose and a black eye. There was also a cigarette burn on the forefinger and a corresponding one on the middle finger of his right hand. The odd part about this incident is that the next day an enormous meteorite was discovered half-buried in the field he had crossed, where it is to be seen to this day. The Indian, however, disappeared.

These are only a few of the mysteries which Nature has up her sleeve to drop down on us if we get fresh and try to stand up straight. In the face of them we ought either to be very humble or else get good and sore.

The
Evil Eye

NEXT to our own system of justice, that in vogue in the interior of Africa has the most laughs in it. They work on the Evil Eye Theory, and the complications that arise from being accused of having the Evil Eye are ludicrous in the extreme.

Mr. MacGregor was accused of having the Evil Eye. that Summer we were in Africa, and my sides ached at the antics he had to go through to prove his innocence. (As a matter of fact, he was guilty, and it cost us plenty to buy the witch doctor, or prosecutor, off.)

*   *   *   *   *

The witch doctor came to me first and told me that I had better get my friend out of town, as several housewives had claimed that he was going around looking at their cooking and spoiling it. (MacGregor had been in trouble several times in America on the same charge.)

I said that our defense would be that the cooking would have been bad anyway, and that this was just an alibi on the part of the house-wives, but the witch doctor said we couldn't get away with that. He said that the only way that MacGregor could prove his innocence would be to walk over red hot stones.

So I went to MacGregor and said:

"There is talk going around town about your having the Evil Eye."

"That's not the Evil Eye," he replied, rubbing it. "That's just hangover. I'm off that native stuff from now on."

*   *   *   *   *

"It's not as simple to explain away as all that," I said. "The witch doctor says that you've got to give proof that you haven't got it."

"Will he come here, or do I have to go to his office?" asked MacGregor, still in the dark as to the seriousness of the accusation.

"All you have to do is go out in the public square and walk over some red hot stones," I explained.

"How far is the public square?" he asked. "I haven't got all day, you know."

"You go right down our street and turn to the left," I said. "They're heating the stones up now. You can leave your shoes here, as you have to go barefoot."

"That's a horse of a different color," said MacGregor, taking off his shoes. "Suppose I get slivers on the way down there?"

"Go down on your bicycle," I suggested.

* * * * *

"It looks to me like a fool's errand," he said. But off he went on his bicycle to the public square, like the old Navy man that he is. I have always said that there's no training for a boy like the Navy.

I stayed at home, as MacGregor had left a lot of work undone (I am always the fall guy who ends up by doing the work around the house), and besides, I wasn't going to stand around and watch MacGregor make a monkey of himself in public.

I was in the middle of a nap when he got back, so he tiptoed around for a while in order not to awaken me. The guy has his sweet side, too. When I woke up I asked him how it went.

"O. K.," he said. "I ad-libbed a little and got some laughs that weren't on the routine." Always clowning, MacGregor is.

"What about the Evil Eye?" I asked.

"Just a little in the right one," he replied.

36

"Nothing that glasses won't correct. What's for supper?"

"Don't make a god of your stomach, Mac-Gregor," I replied.

This got him sore, and he didn't speak until we got back to America.

Stop
Those Hiccoughs!

ANYONE will be glad to admit that he knows nothing about beagling, or the Chinese stock market, or ballistics, but there is not a man or woman alive who does not claim to know how to cure hiccoughs. The funny thing is that the hiccoughs are never cured until they get darned good and ready.

The most modest and unassuming man in the world becomes an arrogant know-it-all in the presence of hiccoughs—in somebody else.

"Don't be silly," he says, patronizingly. "Just put your head under your arm, hold a glass of water against the back of your neck, and count to five hundred by fives without taking a breath. It never fails."

*   *   *   *   *

Then, when it *has* failed, he blames you. "It's absolutely sure-fire if you only follow my directions," he says. He also implies darkly that what is ailing you is not just merely hiccoughs.

"My method can't be expected to cure drunkenness, you know," he says.

To date, I have been advised to perform the following feats to cure hiccoughs:

Bend the body backward until the head touches the floor, and whistle in reverse.

Place the head in a pail of water and inhale twelve times deeply.

Drink a glass of milk from the right hand with the right arm twisted around the neck until the milk enters the mouth from the left side.

Hop, with the feet together, up and down a flight of steps ten times, screaming loudly at each hop.

Roll down a long, inclined lawn, snatching a mouthful of grass up each time the face is downward.

I have tried them all, with resultant torn ligaments, incipient drowning, lockjaw and arsenic poisoning, but, each time, at the finish of the act, and a few seconds of waiting while my mentor says, triumphantly: "See! What did I tell you?" that one, big hiccough always breaks the tension, indicating that the whole performance has been a ghastly flop.

* * * * *

The most unassuming man becomes an arrogant know-it-all in the presence of hiccoughs

My latest fiasco came as the result of reading the prescription of a Boston doctor, and almost resulted in my being put away as an irresponsible person. "All that the sufferer has to do," wrote the doctor, "is to blow up an ordinary paper bag, as if to explode it and then hold it over the mouth and nose tightly, breathing in and out of the bag instead of in and out of the open air."

This, according to the doctor, creates an excess of carbon monoxide gas in the bag, which is breathed over and over again, acting on a nervous center of the brain and curing the hiccoughs.

40

*I blew the bag up and held
it tightly over my face*

Being alone in the room at the time, I blew
the bag up and held in tightly over my face, including not only my mouth and nose, but my
eyes as well, like a gas-mask. I subjected myself to this treatment for possibly three minutes,
walking around the room at the same time to
keep from getting bored.

*   *   *   *   *

When I removed the bag I found myself the
object of the silent but terrified scrutiny of my
wife, who had entered the room without my
knowing it, and who had already motioned for
corroborating witnesses from the next room,

two of whom were standing in the doorway, transfixed.

My explanation that I was curing hiccoughs did not go very big, as what I had obviously been doing was walking around the room alone with a paper bag over my head. This is *not* a good sign.

Incidentally, I still have my hiccoughs.

Bad
News

THERE are certain days when I don't want to hear about certain things. Do you know what I mean?

Today I do not want to hear about fur-bearing trout. The very words "fur-bearing trout" are offensive to me, either in print or in the spoken word. So today I read that a man has reported to the Anglers' Club that he has discovered a fur-bearing trout. That's the way my whole life has been.

At first I thought that I wouldn't read about it. "This is a free country," I said to myself, smiling sadly. "You don't have to read anything you don't want to read. Skip it, and go on to the next page. Keeping abreast of current events is one thing—masochism is another."

* * * * *

But that old New England streak in me, that atavistic yearning for a bad time if a bad time is possible, turned my eyes down into the column which was headed:

FUR-BEARING TROUT AMAZES ANGLERS
Its Pelt Is Called Sure Goitre Cure

And here I am—not only thinking about it but actually writing about it. I may not be able to finish, but here I am, passing the unhappy news on to you.

William C. Adams, director of fish and game activities of the State Conservation Commission of New York, is the authority. Passing up, for the moment, just what fish and game activities call for direction, let us accept Mr. Adams as a man who knows his piscatorial onions. He has everything to lose and nothing to gain by frightening me with a cock-and-bull story about fur-bearing trout. He says:

"Deep in the lakes of Yellowstone, where the waters are so cold they never freeze, looking you straight in the eye, has been discovered this peculiar denizen of the deep. Its fur has been found extremely useful in the prevention of goitre. When collected into a neckpiece the possibilities are unlimited."

* * * * *

This would seem an understatement. The possibilities of a neck-piece made of trout pelts would not only be unlimited—they would be

44

staggering. It could easily drive the wearer crazy, just by her thinking of what she had on. It would start a civil war.

"What is that lovely fur you have on, my dear?"

"That is unborn trout. My husband caught them."

Pistol shots ring out, brother takes up arms against brother, the country dissolves rapidly into chaos.

I feel that such news as this which Mr. Adams brings should be kept from the public. It does no one any good to know that there are such things as fur-bearing trout. If the pelts are good for goitre, let goitre sufferers take advantage of them under another name, such as "piscarin" or "troutoxin." If neckpieces must be made of them, let us go to the French for the *mode* and call them *fourrure de truite*.

But please let's not go about talking of "fur-bearing trout" or "trout pelts." At any rate, not today.

Isn't It
Remarkable?

O N A recent page of colored reproductions
of tomb-paintings and assorted excava-
tions from holes in ancient Egypt there appears
a picture of a goose with the following rather
condescending caption:

> *Remarkably Accurate and Artistic Paint-*
> *ing of a Goose from Pharaoh Akhenaten's*
> *Palace, Drawn 3300 Years Ago.*

What I want to know is—why the "remarkable"? Why is it any more remarkable that
someone drew a goose accurately 3300 years
ago than that someone should do it today? Why
should we be surprised that the people who
built the Pyramids could also draw a goose so
that it looked like a goose?

*   *   *   *   *

As a matter of fact, the goose in this particular picture looks more like a goose than that
of many a modern master. Just what we think
we are. in this age of bad drawing, to call an

Egyptian painting "remarkably accurate and artistic" I don't know, but we have got to get over this feeling that anything that was done correctly in 1000 B. C. was a phenomenon. I say that we have got to get over it, but I don't know how.

People managed to drag along in ancient Egypt, from all that we can gather. They may not have known about chocolate malted milk and opera hats, but, what with one thing and another, they got by. And, presumably, every once in a while somebody felt like drawing a goose. And why not? Is there something exclusively twentieth century about the art of goose-drawing?

We are constantly being surprised that people did things well before we were born. We are constantly remarking on the fact that things are done well by people other than ourselves. "The Japanese are a remarkable little people," we say, as if we were doing them a favor. "He is an Arab, but you ought to hear him play the zither." Why "but"?

*　*　*　*　*

Another thing, possibly not exactly in this connection, but in line with our amazement at obvious things. People are always saying:

"My grandfather is eighty-two and interested in everything. Reads the paper every day and follqws everything."

Why shouldn't he be interested in everything at eighty-two? Why shouldn't he be *especially* interested in everything at eighty-two? What is there so remarkable about his reading the paper every day and being conversant on all topics? If he isn't interested in everything at eighty-two when is he going to be? (I seem to be asking an awful lot of questions. Don't bother answering them, please.)

It is probably this naïve surprise at things that keeps us going. If we took it for granted that the ancient Egyptians could draw a goose accurately, or that Eskimos could sing bass, or that Grandpa should be interested in everything at eighty-two, there wouldn't be anything for us to hang our own superiority on.

And if we couldn't find something to hang our own superiority on we should be sunk. We should be just like the ancient Egyptians, or the Eskimos, or Grandpa.

Do Dreams
Go by Opposites?

TWO or three fishermen have written in asking this department if it believes that dreams go by opposites. I am still trying to tie up their question in some way with fishing, but I can't quite figure it out. I don't even know that they were fishermen.

However, I think that it is safe to say that dreams *do* go by opposites; otherwise, how do you explain the steamboat?

I have a record of a dream in my files which ought to put an end to any doubt on the matter. It was a dream reported to our Dream Clinic by a man who has since settled down and become the father of a family, and, therefore, does not want his name used. (He isn't ashamed of the dream, but the family didn't pan out very well.)

*　　*　　*　　*　　*

According to this man (and there is no reason to doubt his word), he had been worried about business matters for several days preceding the dream, and had decided to just get into bed and pull the covers up around his head. This was around noon.

He had no intention of going to sleep, but, what with one thing and another, he dozed off, and before he could stop himself was dreaming at a great rate. In his dream he was in a large, brilliantly lighted public dining-room with all his clothes on. This, in itself, marks the dream as unusual. He not only had his clothes on, but he was *not* running for a train. This, he thought, was funny, but paid little attention to it at the time.

It seemed to him that he sat fully clothed in this public dining-room, not running for a train —in fact, not doing anything at all for quite a long time, although probably it was for the fraction of a second, really. Then he woke up in a cold sweat. He was so unnerved by this dream that he took off all his clothes, *went* to a public dining-room and *ran* for a train, which was just at that moment leaving the cloak room. He missed it.

Now, here was a dream which worked out in exactly the opposite fashion in his waking experience. This we will call Case A. The man's name will be furnished on request. It was George A. Lomasney.

* * * * *

Case B is almost as strange and equally impressive in proving that dreams go by opposites. A woman was the dreamer in this case (though, aren't we all?) and she is very anxious to give her name, and to waltz with someone, if possible.

In her dream she was in a greenhouse full of exotic plants, which was on a sort of funicular, running up and down the side of a mountain. The mountain was just a shade narrower than the greenhouse, so the ends of the greenhouse jutted out on either side, making it difficult for automobile traffic, which was very heavy at this point, to pass.

In the greenhouse with the woman was a deaf elk which had got in somehow through a hole in the screen. The elk couldn't hear a word that the woman was saying, so she just went on with her tapestry-weaving, as she had to have the job finished before the greenhouse got to the top of the mountain on its 11 o'clock trip. (That is, 11 o'clock from the foot of East Fourteenth street, where it started.)

*   *   *   *   *

Now, the amazing thing about all this was that exactly the opposite thing happened to the woman the very next day. She was *not* in a funicular greenhouse; she did *not* see a deaf elk, and she knew nothing about tapestry-weaving.

Laugh that off, Mr. Scientist!

My White Suit

I HAVE a white suit which I am either going to give away or have dipped. I can't seem quite to swing it.

Other men wear white suits in Summer and it doesn't seem to bother them. But my white suit seems to be a little whiter than theirs. I think also that it may have something written on the back of it, although I can't find it when I take the suit off.

Maybe I don't put it on right. I am sure that all the buttons are buttoned in their proper order, but it doesn't seem to hang as it should. The man who made it for me seemed satisfied, but I think that he was in a hurry to get home. In it I have the feeling of being a sky-writer who can't spell.

I put it on and get as far as the front door, where I catch a glimpse of myself in the mirror. If I didn't know otherwise I would think that I had been wired for electricity and that at eight o'clock the President was going to

I start giggling nervously

press a button lighting me up for the San Diego
Exposition.

*   *   *   *   *

Once out in the daylight I either come back
into the house and change or rush into a taxi
and crouch in the darkest corner. If, through
sheer bravado, I walk, little children run away
whimpering and I feel that policemen are going

to ask me for my hawker's license. The world and I seem to be at cross purposes.

When I see anyone I know coming on the same side of the street I start giggling nervously, and as they come into the picture beat them to it with some such remark as:

"It's white!"

"What's white?" they say, not being in on the secret.

"My suit," I say. "I thought I'd put on a white suit."

"So I see," they say, and into that remark I read anything from mild amusement to downright contempt. Incidentally, on those days when I choose to wear my white suit every other man in the county is dressed in blue serge. This I jot down as a fashion note.

I suppose that such self-consciousness is a form of egotism—that I should think that anyone knows at all what I have on or cares. But that rig is too white; I know that. I have an old brown thing which suits my mood better.

Wear-Out-a-Shoe Week

THERE is a movement on foot to shut down the radio for one evening a week, or one week an evening, so that people will go out on the streets more.

Once they are out on the streets the theory is that they will wear out more shoes, thereby giving employment to 186,000 people in the shoe industry alone. Incidentally they might also drop into a poolroom and help along the chalk industry.

Why are economists always so concerned with shoes? It amounts to fetichism. When they want to make a point it is always illustrated by the number of pairs of shoes that a given number of people will wear out over a given period. Just as in the old arithmetics it was always that A and B were sawing wood or swimming up-stream, in practical economic problems it is always that shoes are being worn out. Doesn't anyone ever care about socks?

* * * * *

"It has been estimated," says Mr. Irving Caesar, in his petition to the Federal Government to shut down the radio occasionally, "that the life of a pair of shoes is 2,500 hours. If fifteen million pairs of shoes have been inactive for one hour it means that the shoe industry has lost fifteen million shoe-hours—and the life of a pair of shoes being 2,500 hours, the shoe industry has lost 6,000 pairs of shoes."

That's an awful lot of shoes to lose. Just think how you feel when the porter doesn't bring *one* pair of shoes back to you in a Pullman, and then multiply that by 6,000. The wonder is that the shoe industry isn't crazy mad.

Personally, shoes do not bother me much. I sometimes just carry mine around with me in a green baize bag and put them on when I want to make a smart appearance. I don't suppose I wear out a pair of shoes in thirty years. I get sick of them and I throw them at pigeons, but I never wear them out. This is because I am what is known as "the sedentary type."

*　　*　　*　　*　　*

If, however, the economic theory back of this move to shut down the radio for one night a week is to make people wear out their shoes, I have an even better plan. Why not let them

57

I put them on when I want to make a smart appearance

stay at home and listen to their old radio if
they want to, but, while they are listening have
them hold a pair of shoes against a grindstone?

58

There is an old Chinese proverb which says: "There are more ways than one to wear out a pair of shoes," and I think it is a very good motto for each and every one of us to take as a guide for our daily lives.

But here again we come to the old problem which worries me so much. Every theory of economic good is based on *my* wearing out shoes, on *my* looking in store windows, on *my* spending money. I have never yet encountered a plan for an economic Utopia which included anyone's reading a piece by Benchley in the paper or even asking Benchley out to dinner. In the Perfect State, Benchley pays.

I suppose it all works out right in the end. I'd be paying anyway. But I resent having it set forth as a dictum.

And, anyway, when I am at home of an evening I don't turn on the radio. I don't wear out my shoes. I am just a parasite—a paying parasite.

Nature's
Noises

THROUGHOUT the ages there have been natural phenomena which have been attributed by the common people (and a few college graduates) to murmurings of the Great Spirit or noisy protests from Valhalla. These have later turned out to be nothing but the cold water faucet dripping into the kitchen sink, or the 11:45 from Portland rumbling over a ledge of rock five miles away.

Some of these queer sounds from lakes and moors have, however, had a deeper significance. They have come from actual convulsions of Nature, and an actual convulsion of Nature is no fun. I know, because I had a relative once who was one.

* * * * *

Take, for instance, the famous "Mumbling Mountain" of Pico, Alaska. Every month or so (excepting February, which has twenty-eight) the inhabitants of Pico heard a loud mumbling like a man talking in his sleep. All of this rapscallion business seemed to come from a nearby mountain, known as Nearby Mountain.

This was naturally attributed to the customary mutterings of the Mountain God, angry because he found himself covered with wet misty clouds. You can hardly blame him. However, thanks to a Dr. Reney, of the Alaska Electric Light and Power Co., it has been discovered that the sounds really came from a new glacier, which was (and still is, unless it has changed its mind) getting ready to start out on a tour of North America. This will make the map of North America look pretty silly, so you'd better not laugh. You wait and see!

*   *   *   *   *

Scientists have, for years, shaken their heads until they ached, over the sound which has come from the skies at Twombley, England. Some of the scientists have said: "Pay no attention to it! You're drunk!" Others have given it as their opinion that it was tops in ominousness. Still others have gone out and got drunk themselves when they heard it.

It has turned out to be simply an echo from the surrounding hills. It is the echo of an old man's voice, screaming. This doesn't help the

61

inhabitants of Twombley much, as you may well imagine, for it has been going on, sporadically, for one hundred and thirty years. The old man shouldn't be screaming that loudly at this late date. A lot of people are still hoping for another explanation.

*　　*　　*　　*　　*

Everyone knows about the "Singing Clam Flats of Garkley," in the outskirts of Gersta, North Wales. On moonlight nights, these clam flats have definitely been heard to hum. Naturally, it was laid to the clams, as Welch miners are great singers, too. In fact, quite a number of Welch clams were taken on a concert tour with a Welchmen's chorus, but they didn't come through as clearly as was expected.

Now, science tells us that these singing clam flats are really not due to clams at all, but the gradual shifting of Wales into Ireland. There has got to be a great deal of bickering before *that* happens, I'll tell you!

So the next time you hear a mountain giggling or a lake bottom turning over on its side, don't just say: "It's the gods who are restless!" You get your things packed up and ask for your hotel bill. Those sounds *mean* something.

Owl
Data

A GRADUATE student in the Ornithology Department of Cornell University is looking for data on horned owls. He is writing a thesis for his doctorate on "Is the Horned Owl a Friend or an Enemy of the Farmer?" and wants people to send in their experiences.

I do not know so much about the farming end of it, but I can testify that the horned owls in my room are definitely unfriendly. I sometimes wish that I had never let them in.

* * * * *

There are only two of them, and so I don't suppose that any extensive conclusions can be drawn. They may just be two particularly unfriendly owls by nature. I, too, may not be doing my part. It takes two or three to make a quarrel. Possibly if I were to throw them a smile now and then they would be more chummy.

But I don't feel like smiling at them. They don't inspire friendliness. They just sit and

63

look at me all night and sleep all day. I have even tried sleeping during the day myself and going out at night, just to get away from their everlasting scrutiny, but that isn't a natural way to live. I can't rearrange my whole life just for a couple of horned owls.

*   *   *   *   *

I asked Mr. MacGregor what to do about them, and he said that he didn't know.

"Is that all you've got to say?" I asked him.

"It's all for the present," he replied. He didn't seem to want to talk about them very much.

"Do you think we'd like them any better if they were stuffed?" I asked.

"No," he said shortly.

So I dropped the subject and tried to forget. The owls were sitting on the top of a bookcase at the time, and I put a screen up in front of them. This helped a little, but it was almost worse at night to look at the screen and know that they were sitting behind there with their eyes wide open, even though I couldn't see them. A couple of nights I even thought I heard them whispering.

*   *   *   *   *

Finally, one day, I said to MacGregor, "I don't think you're doing very much to help this situation."

"What situation is that?" he asked.

"The owl situation," I said.

"Had you thought of moving to another house?" he asked. Mr. MacGregor doesn't sleep here, and so the thing had not reached the proportions in his mind that it had in mine. He has no owls out where he sleeps.

"That's all very well for you to say," I snapped back, my nerves finally giving way, "but how are we going to move the bookcase? Who's going to take the screen down, in the first place?"

"I guess you're right," said MacGregor, and turned and walked away.

That is where the matter stands today. I am afraid that I haven't been able to give much help to the Cornell student, but I *will* give him two horned owls if he wants them—if he will come and get them.

As They Say in French: Other Times, Other Customs

NO MATTER how doggy an institution may be in its beginnings, sooner or later it gets into general circulation. Now they are playing polo in Hollywood and wearing polo coats in the Ozarks.

Some of us older boys can remember back to the days when it was considered putting on the dog to have dinner at night. In New England, at any rate, what was known as "the heavy meal" came in the middle of the day, and anyone who asked you to "dinner" at supper-time would wear lorgnettes.

*　　*　　*　　*　　*

It seems hard to believe now, but the grapefruit was once considered an item of diet which only the president of the Wire Works could have for breakfast. After years and years of being thrown away in Florida as inedible, the grapefruit suddenly took on class. To say to a waiter: "Just bring me a grapefruit first!" marked one as a man of the world and something of a gourmet.

66

The joke about grapefruit squirting in the eye came in shortly after the people who made jokes started blowing themselves to grapefruit. The joke has lasted longer than the prestige of the fruit.

* * * * *

The very word "weekend" was not so long ago used only by Anglophiles. You were going British if you spoke of a "weekend" and you were downright insufferable if you went on one. One of our more classy magazines got its start as a patrician publication by having an article on "Weekending in the Country" every month. A lot of solid, God-fearing Americans wouldn't have the paper on their tables.

And, speaking of affecting British mannerisms and habits, who remembers when cuffs on a man's trousers brought down the jibe: "It's raining in London?" Only "Cholly-off-the-pickleboat" wore white ducks, and, to jump ahead a bit, several prominent citizens today are on record as having once said that they would as soon wear a skirt as a wristwatch.

* * * * *

It was only a few years ago that the fussy traveler had to specify "a room with a bath," and even then did it under his breath for fear that people would think he was on his honey-moon and showing off. Incidentally, the introduction of twin beds into family life was held to be just a touch swanky and possibly an indication that the upper classes were drifting toward an effete civilization.

To step into the next room for a minute, when a man threw in a casual remark about "after my shower this morning" he was quite likely to be under suspicion not only of boasting about a daily bath, but even more of trying to let people know that he was in daily touch with a *shower* bath. The early use of showers by athletes prevented any taint of effeteness, but the owning of a shower was more or less a matter for boasting.

In leaving these erstwhile indications of snobbery, let us ask who remembers when tomato juice in the morning was a sign that a man had been drinking the night before?

Oh, well—*autres temps, autres moeurs*—which, in itself, is a form of affectation. Perhaps. Someday, everyone will be using French phrases.

Help!

A COUPLE of years ago I had occasion to complain of a certain form of California bird-life which was sitting on a tree under my window and making the night hideous by never giving the same bird-call twice. I counted a hundred and four different calls before I went mad, all the calls obviously from the same bird.

But that year I was in a room on the third floor. This year my room is right on the ground, flush with the bushes. And this year that same bird is back with a whole new routine. Furthermore, he is out to get me. And when I say "get me," I mean actual physical violence, or mayhem.

*　　*　　*　　*　　*

He must have read what I wrote about him that time or else some busybody told him. At any rate, he has a definite grudge in mind and has a campaign mapped out whereby he can get me down. His plan is, evidently, to shatter my nerves during the night and then attack me in my weakened condition in the daytime.

Two years ago he had a line of calls which,

I walked by without a word

although diversified, still sounded like a bird. This year he has gone in for *vox humana* numbers. He crowds in against the screen and moans. Sometimes he giggles. Sometimes he simply says, in a low voice, "Wait till I get you outside."

* * * * *

Yesterday, after a night of sitting by the window and shouting "Go away!" I went for a walk in the Petit Trianon back of my house. There

70

was my bird, sitting on a branch, eyeing me. It is an evil black color, with bushy eyebrows and a one-sided leer.

I walked by without a word and tried to act as if I had noticed nothing during the night. But no sooner was my back to him that I heard the whir of wings and felt a heavy body brush by my collar on its way through the air. I ducked, and he banked sharply to the right, circling my head and grazing my other shoulder. I broke into a dignified leap and ran back into the house.

I can see him now, sitting out there on the tree, biding his time. All last night there was a new note of triumph in his program. He has broken my morale and he knows it.

What I want to know is—can I call the police and ask for an escort or has a taxpayer no rights?

Nature's Prizes

AS SOME Frenchman has said, translating at sight into English as he went: "Each one to his taste"; but, with all the things there are to go out after in the world, I think that Dr. Ditmars is going out after the least attractive. At least, they would be to me.

Dr. Ditmars, head of The Bronx Zoo, is going on an expedition to the Caribbean Sea, and, believe it or not, he is hoping and praying that he comes back with the following treasures:

One Surinam toad, which, according to Dr. Ditmars, "looks as if an elephant had stepped on it, and has small beady eyes, like pin-points." This is all right, I suppose, so long as Dr. Ditmars thinks he wants it.

One Giant Horned Frog which attains a length of more than ten inches. "It is bright green, has long yellow horns, barks like a dog, and can inflict a very severe bite. It is apt to jump at you and bite you with no warning whatever." Not at *me*, Dr. Ditmars, not at *me*. He couldn't jump that far.

One tropical spider or *Grammostola lomgi-manca*, which is three times as large as the common tarantula. In addition to being very active, this spider is also very poisonous, and its bite may have a fatal result.

One tree frog of the Harlequin family, highly colored. "Their skins exude a poison which is used by Indians in northeastern South America to tip their arrows. The venom is said to be as deadly as strychnine if it enters the bloodstream, and is fatal within ten minutes."

* * * * *

Now Dr. Ditmars' aim is not to keep as far away from these pets as possible, but actually to go out and *get* them. He wants to bring them back to The Bronx Zoo, although, so far, no residents of The Bronx have issued statements in the matter. It looks like a good year for house screens in The Bronx.

The only one of Dr. Ditmars' quarries which could hold my attention at all is the Surinam toad "which looks as if an elephant had stepped on it." I'd rather like to look at that, and then look right away again.

The Surinam toad also has quite a cute trick in disposing of its eggs. (All this is, of course, according to Dr. Ditmars. It comes like a bolt from the blue to me.) The female lays the eggs in the water, each egg floating by itself. The male then takes them, one by one, in his flipper and imbeds them in the back of the female, where a retaining membrane immediately forms. The young frogs remain on this refuge until they can take care of themselves. More than two hundred eggs have been found on the back of a single female.

*   *   *   *   *

Well, as the Frenchman said, "Each one to his taste." I couldn't go for that sort of thing myself—but then, I couldn't go for any of the other of Dr. Ditmars' hobbies.

Our
Noisy Ghosts

IN AN ill-advised moment last night I began reading an article called *Three Months in a Haunted House*. I merely wanted to find out why anyone would stay three months in a haunted house, or three minutes, for that matter. We are supposedly free agents.

The whole thing ended by my putting on my clothes and going over to spend the rest of the night in the waiting room of the Grand Central Terminal. Even over there I had to ask the man to put on a few more lights. They start cutting down on electricity along about 3 a. m., and it gets a little gloomy.

While I was tagging along at the heels of the cleaning men, from one side of the room to the other, I got to thinking in a more or less sane manner about the difference between modern ghosts and those which haunt castles in Europe, or drift up and down deserted wings of large estates in Scotland. Modern ghosts are so rowdy.

* * * * *

I had to ask the man to put on a few more lights

At just what age does a ghost stop being noisy and throwing things and settle down to dignified haunting? It must have something to do with immaturity in the ghost-world, for only the youngsters seem to take delight in crashing about as if they were drunk. You never hear any of the ghosts in the Tower of London behaving like hoodlums. Of course it may be a matter of breeding.

All accounts of haunted houses today tell of sounds of furniture being thrown downstairs, dishes and spoons being clattered together, and sometimes even actual physical violence, with all the ghosts entering the room and spinning the bed around or yanking off the covers. You would think that Jack Oakie was in the house. Ghosts who have died within the past fifty years all seem to have had grudges against people, or else a tendency to practical joking. They all seem to have been people who, when they were alive, went around pushing other people off rafts into the water, or putting rubber frogs into beer-glasses.

You don't catch any of those nice people who haunt Glamis Castle putting on acts like that. They take a little stroll up and down a corridor or along a battlement; sometimes they just appear at a window for a second and then disappear. Once in a great while they clank a chain or two, but not in a spirit of mischief. You can't help clanking a chain if it is attached to you.

*   *   *   *   *

The chief characteristics of a ghost who has attained a certain amount of dignity are repression and beauty. All the lady ghosts are tall

*I'll bet they wear turtle-neck sweaters
and caps*

and sad, and the men seem to have gone to some good school. Our modern ghosts wouldn't be tolerated in one of those old castles for a minute.

And you will notice that the twentieth-century tin-pan throwers and bed-bouncers never show themselves. If we could see them, I'll bet they wear turtle-necked sweaters and caps. They probably know that once they let anyone catch sight of them they will be so unimpressive that the ghost-racket will be spoiled for them and they will be kicked out into the yard.

Maybe I have gone a little too far. Mind you, I don't say that there can't be ladies and gentle-men among present-day ghosts. I am sure there are. I certainly meant no offense to modern ghosts as a class. They're the ones I'll have to deal with, and I hope that they haven't got me wrong in this little article.

All I meant to say was that times have changed. You know—animal spirits, and boys will be boys. I was really only kidding anyway.

Movie
Boners

ONE of the most popular pastimes among movie fans is picking out mistakes in the details of a picture. It is a good game, because it takes your mind off the picture.

For example (Fr. *par example*) in the picture called "One Night Alone—for a Change," the Prince enters the door of the poolroom in the full regalia of an officer in the Hussars. As we pick him up coming in the door, in the next shot, he has on chaps and a sombrero. Somewhere on the threshold he must have changed. This is just sheer carelessness on the part of the director.

* * * * *

In "We Need a New Title for This," we have seen Jim, when he came to the farm, fall in love with Elsie, although what Elsie does not know is that Jim is really a character from another picture. The old Squire, however, knows all about it and is holding it over Jim, threatening to expose him and have him sent back to the other picture, which is an independent, costing only a hundred thousand dollars.

Now, when Jim tells Elsie that he loves her (and, before this, we have already been told that Elsie has been in New York, working as secretary to a chorus girl who was just about to get the star's part on the opening night) he says that he is a full-blooded Indian, because he knows that Elsie likes Indians. So far, so good.

But in a later sequence, when they strike oil in Elsie's father (in a previous shot we have seen Elsie's father and have learned that he has given an option on himself to a big oil company which is competing with the old Squire, but what the old Squire does not know is that his house is afire) and when Elsie comes to Jim to tell him that she can't marry him, the clock in the sitting room says ten-thirty. When she leaves it says ten-twenty. That would make her interview minus ten minutes long.

*   *   *   *   *

In "Throw Me Away!" the street car conductor is seen haggling with the Morelli gang over the disposition of the body of Artie ("Muskrat") Weeler. In the next shot we see Artie haggling with the street-car conductor over the disposition of the bodies of the Morelli gang. This is sloppy cutting.

In "Dr. Tanner Can't Eat" there is a scene laid in Budapest. There is no such place as Budapest.

What the general public does not know is that these mistakes in detail come from the practice of "block-booking" in the moving picture industry. In "block-booking" a girl, known as the "script-girl," holds the book of the picture and is supposed to check up, at the beginning of each "take" (or "baby-broad"), to see that the actors are the same ones as those in the previous "take."

The confusion comes when the "script-girl" goes out to lunch and goes back to the wrong "set." Thus, we might have one scene in *The Little Minister* where everybody was dressed in the costumes of *The Scarlet Empress*, only *The Little Minister* and *The Scarlet Empress* were made on different "lots" and at different times.

It might happen, even at that.

Let's Not Dance This!

SOMEHOW I do not thrill to the idea that "every form of life is dancing to celestial music," as a well-known but giddy-minded astronomer has stated. Aside from presenting a rather ludicrous picture, it is too tiring to think of. I don't like to dance, and I *won't* dance, celestial music or no celestial music!

It seems as if a greater part of my life has been spent in avoiding dancing. When I was little I used to feign measles and fallen arches on Saturday afternoons when the dreaded time came to put the patent leather pumps into the green baize bag and toddle off to dancing school. I had some pretty clever ruses up my sleeve, but there is no record of their ever having worked.

* * * * *

Incidentally, I believe that the barbarous custom which prevailed at the turn of the century of forcing boys into Saturday afternoon dancing school was responsible for the middle-aged generation of terpsichore-haters whom we see cowering in corners or hitching heavily around dance floors today.

After a Saturday morning of rolling around in the dirt and skinning knee-caps, what red blooded man of eight or nine would not rebel at being called in, given a hot bath in the middle of the day and crowded into a black suit, merely to spend a sunny afternoon indoors with a bunch of girls in blue sashes? It's a wonder that any of us even got married.

Once herded into the torture hall, however, we had ways and means of avoiding the ultimate degradation of actually dancing. Determined groups of stags would barricade themselves in the boys' dressing room and defy adult pleadings until it became a case for calling out the militia. And, even when dragged out into action, there were subtle forms of sabotage such as losing a pump or lacerating the insteps of our partners, which soon broke down the opposition and sent us back to the lockers in triumph.

Following the dancing-school period came the parties where someone, after supper, was always rolling back the rugs and turning on the gramophone. The minute I saw a rug being

*I was out on the porch like a wild,
hunted thing*

so much as turned up at one corner I was out
on the porch like a wild, hunted thing, even
though it was the dead of Winter, and many a
night I have stood jammed against a waterspout
in the dark while searching parties brushed by
me with bloodhounds.

*   *   *   *   *

It wasn't so much that they wanted me to
dance as it was their vicious determination that,
at a party, nobody shall ever be let off anything.
There is no one so unfeeling as a hostess who

is set on having the young folks enjoy them‑selves.

With the years has come that sweet respite from regimentation in matters of merrymaking, and I can now say quite frankly, "Go away, Twinkletoes, and keep away! Grandpa's sitting right here!" Or, better yet, I can get up and give them a taste of their own medicine for one lap around the floor, after which any alterna‑tive that I suggest is greeted with a grateful look and limping acquiescence. But my first in‑stinct is still to rush to the boys' room when I hear the music start.

*   *   *   *   *

So, when astronomers tell us that every form of life is dancing to celestial music and that the earth and the sun set up a rhythm which we cannot escape I settle back in my chair with a confident smile and order scrambled eggs and bacon.

"You go ahead and dance to the celes‑tial music," I say to my group. "I have escaped stronger forces than the earth and the sun in my day. I have braved the thin red line of dis‑approving mothers seated along the wall at dancing school. I have eluded the most eagle‑eyed of hostesses at young people's parties. I

86

have definitely established myself as a non-dancer in some of the dancingest circles of my day. The only time that any celestial influence gets me on my feet will be when it swoops me up for good."

The French,
They Are —

I WAS talking the other day to my friend who happens to be a dachshund about this new restaurant in Paris where they cater exclusively to dogs. It is in the Champs Elysees, a very good location, he tells me, for a smart eating place.

"They call it *Au Colisee*," he said, "although the significance of the name eludes me. I suppose that's the French of it. Hysterical exaggeration." (My friend comes from just outside Munich.)

"I suppose it's all right, if they want to do it," he continued, "but I see no reason for going sissy in it. Look at this!" He read from a menu which some German friend had sent him for his amusement.

"*La Patee de Bouky!* I'll give you ten guesses what *La Patee de Bouky* is. It's soup, rolls and potatoes! That's *La Patee de Bouky!*"

*　　*　　*　　*　　*

He then gave an imitation of an effeminate

dog ordering *La Patee de Bouky*. He overdid it a little, but I got his point.

"Where I come from that dish would be called by a real name—*Kartoffelsuppe mit Brotchen*. There's a name you can get your teeth into! *La Patee de Bouky!* Faugh!"

"The French like to dress things up," I said.

"I don't mind their dressing up," he replied, "but they needn't make a drag out of it. Here's another! . . . *Le Regal de Nica*. Do you know what *Le Regal de Nica* is?"

"I'm sorry, I never tried it," I replied, almost dreading to hear.

"*Le Regal de Nica* turns out to be clear soup, new carrots, and meat ground up very fine. Now, there's a good, sensible dish, fit for any man to eat. But you can't go in and ask for *Le Regal de Nica*, now can you?"

"I don't suppose that French dogs mind it as much as you would," I said. "You have a different background."

* * * * *

"French dogs don't mind *anything*, I have found out," he replied testily. "They even let people put fur pieces on them."

"I noticed you out with a sweater on the other day," I said.

89

"Oh, that old green thing!" he snorted, trying not to show his embarrassment. "I've had that six years. I used to play hockey in it in Germany."

"Hockey or no hockey, you appeared on the street in a sweater. All that I'm trying to prove is that you can't ever judge a man by what he has on."

"Maybe not," said my friend, turning back to his menu to change the subject. "But you can judge a man by what he orders in a restaurant. And I ask you if you would like to hear me ask a waiter for this (*looking up and down the card for something he had evidently been saving as a trump*)—here it is! *La Dessert de Nos Toutous!*"

"*Toutous?*" I asked, incredulously.

"I said *Toutous*," he replied, sneering. "In case you don't know, *Toutou* is a pet name for a dog. It is equivalent to your 'bow-wow,' only less virile. I repeat—would you like to hear me go into a restaurant and order *Dessert de Nos Toutous?*"

"No, I wouldn't," I said, shortly. He won.

Duck, Brothers!

NEXT month will be a bad one for those people who bruise easily, as meteor showers are predicted. It will be well for everyone to travel by subway as much as possible, or, at any rate, to hug up close to the buildings while walking along the street. Those meteors can hurt!

To forestall indignant letters from astronomers and ex-meteors let me say that I know the difference between meteors and meteorites, and that meteorites are the only ones that could hurt if they hit you. But, the way things are going today, it is safe to assume that what would ordinarily be a harmless meteor shower in normal years will end up by being, in this year of grace, a full-fledged rain of ten-ton flame-balls, each one headed directly for the corner of the street on which you and I are standing. I know where I'm not wanted.

*   *   *   *   *

On the map of the heavens I note a group

*Until you see just
what direction it is
taking*

of something called "Delphinus" which has the nickname "Job's Coffin." I have a hunch that my meteorite is coming from "Job's Coffin," straight as a die for the back of my neck. I can feel it now! o-o-o-O-O-O-MMM-ONG-O! And the next thing I know I shall be $MgO:FeO$ or part of an anorthite stick-pin ("Very rare, sir; dug out of a meteorite which fell in the 20th century.")

The best part about a meteorite (I always try to look on the bright side) is that you can hear it coming. The sound has been variously described as that of "the bellowing of oxen," "the roaring of a fire in a chimney" and "the tearing of calico." I certainly hope that mine doesn't sound like the tearing of calico, as that is a sound that drives me crazy. I would almost rather be hit by the meteorite without any warning. (Cross that out, Miss Schwab, please.)

*   *   *   *   *

I suppose that the thing to do when you see a meteorite hurtling through the air at you is to stand like an outfielder until you see just what direction it is taking, and then, instead of running *for* it, run sharply to the right or left. You would have to decide immediately whether it was going to be right or left and *stick to it*, as any attempt at broken-field running would be silly.

You might keep looking up every now and then as you ran, just to make sure that there wasn't a companion piece coming along with the one you were dodging, but the main idea would be to keep running. This is only a tentative plan that I have worked out. I might think up some other scheme on the spur of the moment.

Without being a fatalist, however, I suppose that there isn't much sense in planning ahead on evading a meteorite. If you are going to get hit you are going to get hit, and there's an end to it (which is putting it mildly). The best one can do is keep a stiff upper lip and not let the women folk know that you are worried.

Just the same, I'll be glad when the March meteor showers are over and we can all come out into the open again. Still, I suppose that if it isn't meteorites it will be something else.

What —
No Budapest?

A FEW weeks ago, in this space, I wrote a little treatise on "Movie Boners," in which I tried to follow the popular custom of picking technical flaws in motion pictures, detecting, for example, that when a character enters a room he has on a bow tie and when he leaves it a four-in-hand.

In the course of this fascinating article I wrote: "In the picture called 'Dr. Tanner Can't Eat' there is a scene laid in Budapest. There is no such place as Budapest."

* * * * *

In answer to this I have received the following communication from M. Schwartzer, of New York City:

"Ask for your money back from your geography teacher. There is such a place as Budapest, and it is not a small village, either. Budapest is the capital of Hungary. In case you never heard of Hungary, it is in Europe. Do you know where Europe is? Respectfully yours," etc.

95

I am standing by my guns, Mr. Schwartzer. There is no such place as Budapest. Perhaps you are thinking of Bucharest, and there is no such place as Bucharest, either.

*   *   *   *   *

I gather that *your* geography teacher didn't tell you about the Treaty of Ulm in 1802, in which Budapest was eliminated. By the terms of this treaty (I quote from memory):

"Be it hereby enacted that there shall be no more Budapest. This city has been getting altogether too large lately, and the coffee hasn't been any too good, either. So, no more Budapest is the decree of this conference, and if the residents don't like it they can move to some other place."

This treaty was made at the close of the war of 1805, which was unique in that it began in 1805 and ended in 1802, thereby confusing the contestants so that both sides gave in at once. Budapest was the focal point of the war, as the Slovenes were trying to get rid of it to the Bulgks, and the Bulgks were trying to make the Slovenes keep it. This will explain, Mr. Schwartzer, why there is no such place as Budapest.

*   *   *   *   *

If any word other than mine were needed to convince you that you have made a rather ludicrous mistake in this matter, I will quote from a noted authority on non-existent cities, Dr. Almer Doctor, Pinsk Professor of Obduracy in the university of that name. In his *Vanished Cities of Central Europe* he writes:

"Since 1802 there has been no such place as Budapest. It is too bad, but let's face it!"

Or, again, from *Nerdlinger's Atlas* (revised for the Carnation Show in London in 1921):

"A great many uninformed people look in their atlases for the city of Budapest and complain to us when they cannot find it. Let us take this opportunity to make it clear that there is no such place as Budapest and has not been since 1802. The spot which was once known as Budapest is now known as the Danube River, by Strauss."

*   *   *   *   *

I would not rebuke you so publicly, Mr. Schwartzer, had it not been for that crack of yours about my geography teacher. My geography teacher was a very fine woman and later became the mother of four bouncing boys, two

97

of whom are still bouncing. She knew about what happened to Budapest, and she made no bones about it.

In future communications with me I will thank you to keep her name out of this brawl.

MacGregor for Ataman!

WHAT is the news this morning, Mr. Mac-
Gregor?" I asked, peering around from
behind a hangover. "Just give me the key-
words."

"It says here," replied MacGregor, catering
to my whim, "that the Don Cossacks who have
been exiled in this country since the Russian
revolution are going to elect a new Ataman
this month."

"I know why you read me that item," I
countered, and got the desired answer: "Why?"

"So that you could say 'At-a-man!' "

MacGregor blushed furiously.

"Go ahead and say it anyway," I said, my gen-
erous side coming to the fore.

"At-a-man!" murmured MacGregor, making
believe he hadn't said it.

*   *   *   *   *

"And now I have a surprise for you!" I said,
getting up off the floor. "*You* are going to be a
candidate for the office of Cossack Ataman!"

"But I am not a Cossack," protested Mac-Gregor, weakening.

"You have the spirit of a Cossack," I replied. "With boots and a sabre and a Persian lamb hat you could ride down peasants in the grand manner."

"I don't think so," he said, ruminatively. "And besides, I couldn't run for Ataman right now. We have too much work piled up here in the planetarium."

" 'The work can wait,' " I said, quoting our business motto. "I am backing you for Cossack Ataman, and you would do well not to look a gift horse in the mouth."

* * * * *

"What do I have to do to get votes?" asked MacGregor, pulling on his mittens.

"Just go around among the exiled Cossacks in town," I explained, "and tell them that you are a candidate. Threaten them, if necessary."

"With what?" he asked.

"Just glare at them," I said.

"How's this?" asked MacGregor, glaring.

"Another rehearsal and you'll have it down cold," I said, although I had my doubts.

But I'll be darned if MacGregor didn't go out and get enough votes to be elected.

Do We Sleep Enough?

DOES the average man get enough sleep? What is enough sleep? What is the average man? What is "does"?

It is said that Napoleon was able to go for days without sleep and then make up for it with a sleep of twenty-four hours' duration. The temptation is to say "And look at Napoleon now!" but that would be not only an old-fashioned crack but an irrelevant one. Napoleon happens to be doing all right now, in a bigger tomb than any of us sleepy-heads will ever get.

Some people claim that they can do with four hours' sleep, without explaining what they mean by "do with." Do what with? I can do all kinds of things with fifteen minutes' sleep, including gagging, snorting and getting my head caught between the couch and the wall, but don't boast about it.

Napoleon is said to have . . . Sorry!

* * * * *

A man who goes to bed, let us say, at seven in

the evening, or even seven-fifteen, can get his eight hours' sleep and still have from three a. m. (or 3:15 a. m.) on to do what he wants in. He can milk cows, cut ice, or, if he happens to live in New York, go up to Harlem for the early show. Then there are always long walks in the country.

But even eight hours' sleep do not do any good if they are spent wondering what it is that is lying across the foot of the bed just over your ankles. Unfortunately I am without a dog at present, so there is no way for me to explain to myself what it is that lies across my ankles just after I get to sleep. All that I can do is hope that it is someone that I know.

* * * * *

There are several different schools in the question of what position is the most restful during sleep. Some claim that one arm should be wrapped around the head (to keep curiosity-seekers from discovering who is in the bed) and the other extended backward so that the hand clutches the electric-light switch, in case screamers or chain-rattlers get into the room. This leaves the feet to be arranged at the pleasure of the sleeper.

Others are convinced that a really recupera-tive night can be spent only by sitting bolt up-right in bed, with the eyes open and a large blunderbuss across the knees. In this proposi-tion it is best to keep the lights on, as clicking them on and off constantly makes quite a racket which is likely to disturb the sleeper.

I, personally, like to sleep with my head out the window and my feet in a tepid foot-bath (72 degrees). Thus I am able to watch up and down the street and, at the same time, draw the circulation away from my head, where it is so unhappy.

*　　*　　*　　*　　*

Infants need the most sleep, and, what is more, get it. Stunning them with a soft, padded hammer is the best way to insure their getting it at the right times.

As a person gets older he needs less and less sleep, until by the time he is ninety-five or a hundred it doesn't make any difference whether he gets any sleep at all. This scientific fact ac-counts for the number of nonagenarians one sees on the street at three and four in the morn-ing. Or maybe it is just that they *look* like nonagenarians.

The best way to induce sleep is to take off all the clothes, get into some comfortable sleeping garment and lie down in bed. You can then always get up, put on some comfortable hunting togs and go out and run down a fox.

High Life
Among the Birds

BEING terrified of birds myself, I have, naturally, a morbid interest in all their more horrendous activities. It is a form of masochism in which the patient suffering from "aviaphobia" actually *seeks out* bird-shocks, and asks people questions about the most revolting birds they have known.

It was with considerable revulsion and consequent excitement, therefore, that I read in Mr. D. B. Wyndham Lewis' column in the *London Daily Mail* of a recent bird debauch in England which must give pause to even the most sanguine of bird-lovers.

(Mr. D. B. Wyndham Lewis, by the way, is one of the few remaining madmen of the bulldog breed, and is not, by even the most literate, to be confused with the other Wyndham Lewis, who, so far as I have ever been able to ascertain, has never had more than a sober thought in his head.)

* * * * *

"By an unfortunate oversight," writes Mr. *D. B.* Wyndham Lewis, "a bird-lover of my acquaintance replenished the bird bath in his lawn the other evening from a jug of melted ice in which lingered a few cocktail dregs.

"The birds," he said, "mopped it up avidly and swarmed around shouting for more; and at length there was great excitement and babbling in the trees, with bursts of sardonic laughter. My friend who has an ear for bird talk, overheard a truculent blackbird proposing to fly to Kensington and peck the stuffing out of Peter Pan, and a very noisy nightingale boasting at the top of its voice that 'we microphone artists' could lay an egg in Sir John Reith's hat any old time, and nothing said.

"In a word," he said, "it was just like any other cocktail party except that nobody fell down."

* * * * *

If Mr. D. B. Wyndham Lewis had not brought the matter up in his succinct summary I should probably have kept my promise never to mention the occasion on which two guinea hens of my acquaintance made perfect fools of themselves through liquor. They apologized the next day, and I said to forget it. However, as I have since learned that the guinea hens in question ended up in an asylum, I have no compunctions now.

It came about through a spilled keg of hard cider, but, so far as I know, that has never been an excuse. The guinea hens got drunk. We might as well face it. They were drunk.

My fear of birds increases in direct proportion to their personality. Birds who mind their own business find me very tractable, but a bird who sets out to impress me soon learns that he has the police to deal with. I am incapable of handling the affair myself, but I know where to go for help.

*   *   *   *   *

These two guinea hens, once they realized their advantage, deliberately set out to hector me. They were like two drunken "townies" hanging around the drug store as unprotected girls go by. First, they annoyed me with remarks; then they actually set in motion after me and tried to trip me up. One of them even left the ground and struck me on the hip, while the other laughed coarsely.

I am frank to admit that I ran into the barn and told on them. I said to the man in there: "Has it got so that a man of forty can't walk through your barnyard without being attacked by drunks?" Then I went into the harness room until the scene was over.

As I say, they apologized the next day, but I want Mr. D. B. Wyndham Lewis to know that we, in America, have our problems of drunkenness among birds, too. In England they seem to carry their liquor better, that's all.

Do You
Make These Mistakes?

A GREAT many people use faulty English without knowing it. Ain't you?

How many times, for instance, have you wanted to use the word "eleemosynary" and haven't been able to do so without laughing? So you have used "whom" instead, thinking that it means the same thing. Well, it don't—doesn't.

Probably one of the most prolific causes of mistakes in spoken English is the use of intoxicating liquors. "Impftubbibble" is not good English, and you know it. Neither is "washerti'?" And yet you hear educated people say these words in the best circles, and think nothing of it. It is merely a slovenly way of speaking, induced by an even more slovenly way of drinking.

*   *   *   *   *

The English language is derived from the Latin, Greek, French, Saxon, Spanish and Yiddish. That is why English is such a difficult lan-

*"Impftubbibble" is not
good English*

guage for foreigners to learn. Arabs and Turks
are completely at sea with it.

But there is no reason why you should be at
sea. All that is needed is a few hours' practice
every day, being careful not to bend the knees.
Just keep saying to yourself, over and over
again, "I *shall* speak good English!" Before
long, you will find yourself saying: "I *will* speak
good English!" or possibly just: "The hell with
it!"

Try taking a pencil and jotting down the
number of times during the day that you find
yourself making the following common mistakes in everyday English:

I didn't ought to have went.

Whom am I? (for where am I).

Sure, I'll sign! What is it?

My private telephone number is Bogardus 9-476. (This is a very common mistake.)

Heil Hitler!

Id vork geleddi ompta id imny. (The worst English imaginable.)

You may think that these little slips, and others like them, do not matter in ordinary conversation. "I make myself understood, don't I?" you may say. Ah, but do you?

* * * * *

Napoleon failed to take Moscow until it was a mass of ruins because he said: "Take your time, Joe!" instead of "Hurry up, Joe!" to the man who had charge of the army. Just the difference of three little words.

A man in Colorado was hanged for murder because in a written statement he said, "I did it," instead of "I didn't do it." If he had known the most elementary rudiments of English he wouldn't have made such a monkey of himself.

If I had known the most elementary rudiments of English I wouldn't have written "the most elementary rudiments." So you see?

The Word "Three"

I DON'T know whether you care or not, but etymological circles are in an uproar. They have just discovered what the word "three" comes from.

They have known the derivation of all the other words in the number-table (as, for example, "two" from "Tuesday," or the second day in the week if you don't count Sunday as the first, and "five" from the god Woden, or Thor, or Buttercup, and so forth and so forth), but they have never been able to figure out where the word "three" came from.

*　　*　　*　　*　　*

A little fellow from the University of Welf discovered it. He doesn't speak English himself, but he is awfully interested in people who do. It was during one of these periods (I should have told you that he has periods when he looks up words) that he found out about the word "three." He was looking up the word "tree" and, not speaking English well, he thought that it was pronounced "three." You can see how that might very well be.

The word "three" comes to us direct from the French, collect. The original word was (and still is) *tri*, which means a sorting, or, as in card-playing, a deal. Thus, one would say: "Give me a *tri*," or "How is your *tri*?" meaning "Give me a deal" or "How is your deal?" If one were really speaking in French, of course, all the other words in the sentence would be French, too. (i.e., *"Donnez-moi un tri"* or *"Votre tri, ça marche?"*)

Just how the word *tri* got into the French language is a mystery which occupies practically nobody's attention at the moment. It is supposed to have come from the Creole patois of New Orleans, and was used to signify hurry or lethargy. The old form of the word was *blo*, which gradually was shortened into *tri*. Later the whole word was dropped from the language by a rising vote.

*　　*　　*　　*　　*

The Normans brought the word into England just before the Norman Conquest. In their use of it an extra syllable was added, making it *triouille*, meaning white-bait or Roger crab. We still are no nearer than we were to finding out

113

how it came to mean three of anything. Don't think that I'm not just as worried as you are.

With the advent of water-power and the subsequent water-pistol, Luke (Luke was the fellow I was speaking of a few yards back) didn't know what to do. Unless I am greatly mistaken, this paragraph belongs in another article.

Well, anyway, the people who are making up the English language found themselves with names for every digit except "three." And, as there were three of quite a lot of things (Marx Brothers, blind mice, wishes and cent stamps) it got increasingly embarrassing not to have a word to express "three." They tried using the word "four," but it ended only in confusion, especially when addition or subtraction was at stake.

*   *   *   *   *

Suddenly someone said: "Why don't we take the word *tri* from the French? They'll never miss it, and they owe it to us anyway." This seemed like a logical plan, and everybody but one man agreed to it. He later committed suicide when he found out how successfully it had worked out. "I was a blind fool," he wrote.

As it sounded rather common to say *tri*, they put in an *h* and substituted a double *e* for the *i*.

This made as pretty a "three" as you could wish, and from that day on it was a part of the language. They tried it out in a little rhyme: "One-two-three—buckle my shoe," and it went so well that soon everybody was saying it.

Frankly, I don't know whether I like it as a word or not. It still sounds a little slangy.

Read
and Eat

I HAVE always secretly admired people who could read a newspaper while eating. It bespeaks co-ordination, dexterity and automatic digestion, none of which attributes I seem to possess. It also gives one an air of being a man of affairs, and I long ago abandoned the attempt to look like a man of affairs. I even find it difficult, some mornings, to look like a man.

In the first place, I can't seem to get the newspaper fixed right, even in one of those racks which super-service hotels sometimes provide for the purpose. One corner gets into the butter, another into the marmalade, and, even if I do manage to fold it so that certain headlines are visible, they are either on stories that I don't want to read or I have to unfold the whole thing again in a minute or two in order to keep on reading.

* * * * *

In the meantime, what of breakfast? I like my breakfast, and I like it hot. A cold egg is

*I can't seem to get the
newspaper fixed right*

like a pretty good curate. While I am balancing my newspaper, and folding it and unfolding it, and knocking over cream pitchers and salt cellars, and getting everything set to read two paragraphs of a full column story, the Grim Reaper has stalked in among my breakfast dishes, laying his icy hand on egg and muffin alike. There is no news story in the world that is worth that.

Let us say, however, that I have finally found a story that holds my attention, that enough of it is exposed to view to be read consecutively for two minutes, and that I have taken a bite of bacon and toast. I read, and, as I read, I chew, leaning over at an angle to the left, so that my lapel rests neatly in the egg.

It is my particular misfortune to be unable to do all these things at the same time. If a point in my story fascinates me I stop chewing.

117

*I grope tentatively for my
coffee cup*

If I don't actually stop chewing I go ahead automatically, with no relish for the food, and might as well be saving money and chewing on a rubber washer. It is a dull, stolid mockery of eating, blessing neither him that gives nor him that takes.

*　　*　　*　　*　　*

If the story continues interesting I keep my eyes glued on the paper and grope tentatively for my coffee cup. I know that it should be near my right hand, but, beyond that, I am willing to try out any old location. I dip my fingers, first, lightly on the edge of the toast-dish; next, like a butterfly alighting, on the rim of my water glass; then, as if by intuition, directly into the coffee itself. This brings me to my senses, and I take my eyes from the newspaper and go about my business, which, after all, is eating my breakfast.

118

Others, more dexterous than I, may be able to swing both reading and eating at the same time. I am more the *gourmet* type and like my food. If the breakfast is good—and most breakfasts are—I prefer to concentrate on that and let my newspaper reading go until later.

Of course, there are mornings when I don't want any breakfast. Then I can catch up on my reading.

Talking Dogs

THERE is a story going the rounds of a man who was driving a horse up hill with a heavy load, his dog running along beside the wagon.

Suddenly the horse stopped short in his tracks and spoke: "Listen! I'm sick of this!" he said. "I don't pull this load another step."

"Well, I'll be darned!" said the man, taken aback. "I never heard a horse talk before."

"Neither did I," said the dog.

Now, this story may seem a little fantastic to the layman, but, from the data that I have been able to gather, the thing is not beyond the realm of possibility. At any rate, not the dog's end of it. The man's remark seems a little far-fetched.

* * * * *

There was a 12-year-old Great Dane named "Boulderwall" who died a few years ago in Rhode Island. She could make herself understood, according to the report, "to a limited extent," by intoning her "bow-wow and r-r-ow." It didn't say to whom she could make herself understood, but it must have been an awfully nice person—or a heavy drinker.

Thus, when Boulderwall wanted water, she said: "Wow-r-r." That's better than a lot of us are able to do at times. I would have liked to try her out on "two two-and-a-half-minute eggs," but possibly she didn't like eggs. When "wow-r-r-r" is the best you can do for "water," you're not likely to be eating much, anyway.

* * * * *

The most famous talking dog was "Princess Jacqueline" (they all seem to have been ladies), a French bull who lived in Maine. The Princess had a vocabulary of about twenty words which she could form into sentences. This I definitely would *not* have cared to hear. One word, yes, but a whole sentence and I might be tempted to drop whatever I was doing and leave the room by the window. I'm no fool, as the fellow said.

A conversation between Boulderwall and Princess Jacqueline might have been interesting to listen in on, provided you happened to be feeling in tip-top shape yourself that day. Boulderwall had the size but the Princess had the vocabulary, so, unless the thing degenerated into a brawl, the odds would have been on the Princess to get her point across.

I had a dog once who could sing *Come, Josephine, in My Flying Machine,* but I had to get rid of him. (This is the first time I have ever told anyone about it.) He flatted badly on the "up she goes!" and that sort of thing gets on one's nerves after a while.

I still like taciturn dogs better than the gabby kind.

My
Trouble

WHAT is it, do you suppose, when your throat closes up and you stop breathing? Am I a victim of an inferiority complex?

I am a boy of 46, partly white, and stand in my stocking feet. I haven't had a drink since Repeal, as I believe in the Constitution. (I did have something made from potatoes, a white liquid which my old Russian nurse called wodka, but it didn't seem to have any effect. A-ha-ha-ha-ha-hee!)

Now it turns out that, when I lie down to go to sleep, my throat closes up and I stop breathing. This idiosyncrasy brings me, like a flash, out of bed and onto my feet in the middle of the floor, looking for the electric light. (We have had electric lights ever since they were invented, although we are thinking now of going back to gas.)

*   *   *   *   *

What I want to know is—am I unusual for my age? Do all boys of 46 stop breathing when they go to bed? Should I see a specialist?

Brings one out of bed looking for the electric light

When I first noticed that I wasn't breathing I paid no attention to it, thinking that it was a figment of my imagination. "Of course you're breathing," I said to myself, gasping for breath, "look at your clothes over the chair there! Those aren't the clothes of a man who isn't breathing." This reassured me for a while. I even got up and put on my clothes and walked, very fast, to the City Line, taking the trolley back.

124

Then I began to think: "Who are you to say that you are breathing when you're not?" I had no answer to this. I had evidently got in over my depth. When you can't answer your own questions it is time to stop.

* * * * *

I took my case to a psychoanalyst. "I stop breathing when I lie down," I said, smiling. "What is that?"

"It is a form of jumpiness," he said. "You stop breathing when you lie down."

"I know that," I said. "I was the one who told you."

"That's right, I guess you were," said the psychoanalyst.

"All I want to know is—what is it?" I insisted. (I am an insisting cuss.)

"You have a phobia," he said. "You are afraid of stopping breathing when you lie down."

"Well, I'll be a son-of-a-gun," I said. "You certainly have hit the nail on the head. Just watch me!" So I lay down and stopped breathing.

"See—what did I tell you?" he said.

* * * * *

This sobered me for a minute. The psycho-analyst took it in his stride.

"All that you need to do," he said, "is to breathe when you lie down."

"You mean inhale and exhale?" I asked.

"That's one way of putting it," he said, smiling tolerantly.

"I guess you're right at that," I said. "Just inhale and exhale."

"When you are lying down," he added.

"Ah—there's the catch," I replied, catching.

"You are just making things more difficult for yourself," he said. "Go home, and come back to me tomorrow."

"I not only won't come back to you tomorrow," I said, "but I won't go home."

I still want to know what it is when your throat closes up and you stop breathing when you lie down.

Hollywood's Loss

AS A movie actor, I pride myself on being untemperamental and easy to work with, but there are some things that an artist simply cannot take. One of them is a puppy who wants to hog every scene.

I have been working in a picture (contemptuously known in the trade as a "short subject") in which it was unfortunately necessary to employ a Scottie pup. He was more or less intended as a "straight man" for me. He doesn't even rate second billing. He is just an extra, when you come right down to it.

The trouble was that he didn't know his place. He thought that he was the star. I don't mind sharing a scene with another actor. In fact, I often step aside and let others take the limelight—if I feel that it is for the good of the picture. I will not, however, be imposed upon.

This particular dog has had no picture training. In fact, he has had no training at all, being in the neighborhood of two months old. He was

127

hired for the part simply because of his size, which is negligible. We wanted a dog who would look futile, and he seemed, at the time, to fill the bill.

*   *   *   *   *

He turned actor on me, however. Once on the set, he became insufferable. Every scene that we had together he crabbed by backing me up-stage, "catching flies" (the theatrical term, meaning to distract attention from the speaker) and even walking right off the scene during my big speeches. At the age of two months, he knew more tricks of scene stealing than a stock company actor.

I finally complained to the director—something that I have never had to do before. I simply said: "Choose between this newcomer and me. Either he gives me common courtesy during my scenes, or I walk out."

The director took the matter to the Front Office and they had a conference on it. The result was that I was informed that they felt that they had a "find" in the puppy, and that I could do as I liked.

I just want it understood why I am leaving

the motion picture business. I will not play "straight" to a Scottie puppy, and I don't feel that I am being unreasonable.

From now on these dispatches will be dated "New York."

Lights, Please!

OH, DEAR, now they've gone and discovered a woman who lights up! And just as things were getting back to normal again! Why can't they stop poking around?

The story of this "luminous woman" appears in the *London Illustrated News*, so it can't be a publicity gag. They've got a whole page about her, taken from *L'Illustrazione Italiana*, with charts and spectra and a cute photograph of Mrs. Anna Monaro, who is the eccentric lady in question.

Mrs. Monaro lives in Pirano, Italy, and lights up only at intervals. She doesn't keep glowing all the time, but they haven't got her perfected yet. Think how long it took Edison to get his electric bulb to working. When they get Mrs. Monaro so that she will give off a steady light Mussolini is going to press a button from Rome to start the grand illumination.

* * * * *

People sleeping in the room with Mrs. Monaro (and, oddly enough, *Mr.* Monaro doesn't seem to figure in the testimony, although, of course it's none of my business. Mr. Monaro is a fisherman who takes long trips), were the first to notice the phenomenon. While asleep, Mrs. Monaro gave off a light from her thorax. You may well imagine that there was little more sleeping done in that room that night. Italians are so excitable.

Doctors and priests and a man from the electric light company were rushed to Pirano, and the humble fisherman's wife became the center of scientific discussion, first, over all Italy, then over all Europe, and now on this page. The discussion on this page, however, will probably give you less idea of just what goes on in Mrs. Monaro's thorax than the scientific discussions in Europe. I frankly am still pretty much in the dark about it.

*   *   *   *   *

They put "Miss Electricity 1934" under observation, and found that her little spells occur only when she is asleep, which makes it rather tough for her, as she can't look down and see it. Maybe it is just as well. I could do without that little excitement if I were Mrs. Monaro.

The doctors have decided, rather half-heartedly, that she is of such a highly sensitive nature that, when she has been emotionally upset during the day, her visceral functions are unbalanced, her combustion is increased and the radiating power of the blood given a terrific boost. So far I understand what they are saying, but ——

Mrs. Monaro, being very religious, also does a lot of fasting, "which promotes the concentration of sulphides, which, although normally opaque, become luminous when struck by the ultra-violet radiations of the blood."

The doctors add that "given propitious experimental conditions, the phenomenon might be reproduced artificially."

Not in me, it won't be! I'll stick to the old-fashioned electric light, thank you.

Did You Know That

DID you know that:

Ice is really not ice at all, but a vegetable organism which forms on the surface of water to *prevent* it from freezing solid?

An ordinary hen's egg is the result of hypnotism?

If you take a ton of anthracite coal (ordinary anthracite) and press it, you can use it as "pressed anthracite" for blacking up in minstrel shows?

Mount Washington, of the Presidential Range, is really a depression in the earth's surface which looks high only because the surrounding country is so much lower?

The great general Hannibal was really a woman, and a five-foot-two woman at that?

One year's supply of that other condiment that comes in the second jar on a horse-radish cruet, would not cover one square foot of a city the size of Rochester, N. Y.?

No one has ever actually *seen* Brooklyn Bridge? It is merely an action of light waves on the retina of the eye.

Eel-grass, such as is now used to entangle oars, was once a delicacy in Egypt?

If you were to inhale steadily for fifteen minutes, without once exhaling, your head would touch the floor in back of you?

Frederick the Great once gave a walking stick to Voltaire which bent double every time he leaned his weight on it, which was the reason that Voltaire was such a cynic?

The reason why it always says "twenty minutes past eight" on those big watches that hang outside jewelers' shops is because that is actually the time at the particular moment when you are looking at it?

*   *   *   *   *

These and four hundred thousand other fascinating facts, you will find in a little booklet called *How to Roll a Hoop*, which I am preparing for a few friends as a birthday surprise to myself. I am verifying each fact as I write it in, which explains why it is taking me such a terribly long time to get the booklet out.

Or hadn't you noticed that it *was* taking me a long time?

Mutiny on the "Bounty"

"I F WE had a goat," I said to Mr. MacGregor, "it would solve all our problems."

"A what?" he asked, without looking up.

"A goat," I repeated.

"It would solve what?" he asked again, still marking down figures.

"All our problems." (He evidently hadn't heard anything I said the first time except the words "would solve.")

There was quite a long silence during which Mr. MacGregor went out and bought some sport shirts. I tended shop.

When he came back he walked straight through the office with his bundle and into the planetarium.

"Who would take care of the goat?" he finally asked, from the other room.

"Well," I replied, "technically it would come in your department—Public Works. I would take it over, however, on any day when you might be sick or nervous. You would find me very willing to help, I assure you."

He said no more, but I heard a sound of clicking once, like suitcase snaps being snapped. It seemed a little odd that MacGregor should be in there snapping suitcase snaps, so I dismissed it as an improbability. "It is most likely just the wind," I thought.

* * * * *

However, hearing nothing for several hours after that, I went into the planetarium. It was empty. Mr. MacGregor had left by the door leading into the Rose Bowl.

On the table was a note. "I am running away from home," it read, "to go to sea." The old Navy urge had been too strong for him.

I was a little hurt, but disgust was predominant in my mind. Loyalty to me, the amassing of a great fortune from the business, his brown hat (which he had left in the front office), all these meant nothing to him. Obviously the man was incompetent.

Within two hours private detectives (paid out of my own pocket) had him back in the office again. They had found him just as he was enlisting.

I thought it best not to say anything about his escapade. He seemed a little subdued.

"About that goat," I said. "When we get it ——"

"I bought a goat on the way home from the recruiting station," said Mr. MacGregor. "He's out in the car."

So everything worked out all right.

The Dangers
of Bass-Singing

A GREAT many people wish that they could sing bass. In fact, a great many people think that they *are* singing bass when what they are really doing is growling the air an octave or two below the rest of the group. A really good bass is the hardest drunk to find.

And yet, how many people know the dangers which confront a bass-singer? The occupational diseases known to insurance companies as "the basso-profundo risk"—what of them? One must pay the penalty for singing bass just as for all the other pleasures of the flesh.

In the first place, you are likely to get your chin caught underneath the knot of your necktie. This is no simple matter to set aright. I knew of a man once who, on the three final "zum-zum-zum's" of "Kaintucky Babe," got what they call "cast," in horse parlance, and had to be carried, with his chin tucked in his collar, all the way from the boat-house, where he was singing, to a blacksmith's shop.

*   *   *   *   *

You are likely to
get your chin
caught

Several years ago a picture appeared in *Punch* which showed an elderly, benevolent gentleman stopping in front of a group of small boys who seemed to be singing Christmas carols. The smallest of the waifs (and he was so small as to be hardly worth including in the picture at all) was holding his handkerchief to his face in evident distress.

"What is the matter, my little man?" asked the old gentleman, in the manner of old gentlemen in *Punch* pictures. "Why are you crying?"

" 'E's not cryin'," replied the leader of the

carolers. " 'E just tried to sing bass and it made 'is nose bleed."

Now that may seem a very funny joke to you (or it may not, but if it doesn't, never darken my door again), but it represents without a doubt one of the things which a bass-singer has got to watch out for. A rupture of the delicate membranes of the nose and throat, or a too great strain put upon the blood vessels, and bass-singing can transform a place into a shambles.

* * * * *

The eyes, too, come in for their share of punishment. In executing a really good descent into the lower register the eyes must either be closed (by far the safest method) or rolled back into the head as the brow goes forward. If the singer persists in looking at his audience while his chin is in his collar he is running the risk of permanent dislocation of the eyeballs, which will give him a rather horrid look when he raises his head again.

Among other ills to which the bass-singer is heir are "chest-mouse," caused by teeth dropping into the chest at the lowest note and staying there; "ascending larynx," which means, that as the other organs are lowered the larynx remains constant, giving it the effect of rising into the throat and choking the operator; and actual Death, or Hoxie's Disease, caused by the stoppage of all functions except that of bass-singing.

The question is: "Is it worth it?"

Lucky World!

WHEN you come to think of it, the wonder is not that there are so many jammed automobile fenders, bad motion pictures, sore throats, divorces and wars, but that there aren't *more* of them. We are living in a world that is shot through with luck, that's all.

The next time you are up in a tall building looking for a place to jump from, just take a peek over at a couple of busy traffic intersections below. Then figure out how many of those drivers should be at large on the street at all, much less at the wheel of an automobile. Then make your jump.

*   *   *   *   *

When you consider that the world is full of men who can't stoop over to tie their shoes without bumping their heads, women to whom left and right are interchangeable as a matter of principle, young people whose parents are still wondering when they are going to develop mentally beyond the age of nine—all driving automobiles—then the logical ending to the whole situation is for all the automobiles in the world to pile up on top of one another at one big cross-road.

I, myself, am aghast at the possibilities of such a catastrophe when I think of what might happen in my own case if Nature really took its course when I am at the wheel, and there must be millions of people driving who are no better equipped than I am to guide a motor vehicle through any more of an emergency than a sudden light breeze.

When I consider what would result in the way of pictorial entertainment if I, myself, were asked to direct, photograph, cut or supervise a motion picture, I marvel at the success with which thousands of other people, many of them in my class, turn out pictures which actually hang together, make some sense, and show up on a screen. It amounts to a phenomenon not without the suspicion of black magic.

* * * * *

Consider the number of young people all over the world who are getting married, day in and day out, for no other reason than that someone of the opposite sex looks well in a green jersey or sings baritone, and then tell me that Divorce has reached menacing proportions. The surface of Divorce has not been scratched yet. We are lucky that *everyone* isn't divorced.

Look at the people in the Congress, or the Chamber of Deputies, or the Parliament in London, and listen to what they say. The only logical ending to it all is that the world is headed for *dementia præcox*, with all the buildings tumbling down, all the water works shooting up into the air and all the citizens bumping into each other with trays of hot soup.

And yet automobiles dodge each other as if by magic, passable motion pictures are produced, many people stay married all their lives and actually don't seem to mind, and only occasionally does hell break loose entirely.

* * * * *

It's a pretty lucky old world we live in, when you consider its possibilities.

"Name, Please?"

IN READING books about Russians or the ancient Romans, there is an extra hazard which makes the going very difficult for us old plodders. The names of the characters don't mean a thing.

For example, a Roman Emperor's name may have been Tiberius Claudius Drusus Nero Germanicus (it was, as a matter of fact), which gave quite a lot of leeway for anyone who wanted to call him quickly. The only trouble was that his uncle's name was Tiberius, and his brother's name was Germanicus, and his successor's name was Nero, all probably ending in the other four names.

A Russian character's name could very well be Stepan Nikolaevitch Gubaryov, and he be called Grisha, which is the nickname for Gregory. Or sometimes he is called Stepan, sometimes Nickolaevitch, sometimes Gubaryov, or sometimes just Pishtchalkin, meaning "Boy with the Long Ear Lobes."

* * * * *

145

It would be only poetic justice if a bunch of Russians should find themselves in a novel about ancient Rome. Confusion would be, for the moment, rife.

Vasily Ivanovitch Popof Tchitchorna Grushenkov comes to see Caius Gallus Drusus Postumus Galba on business.

"May I speak to Gallus?" he asks the secretary.

"What name shall I say?" asks the secretary.

"Popof," he replies.

In a few minutes the secretary announces: "Drusus will see you now!"

"I said I wanted to see Gallus."

"That's Drusus."

"Gallus is Drusus, eh? That's fine! Oh, and, by the way, if a call comes for Grushenkov, please tell them that I am here and will be leaving in about half an hour."

"I beg your pardon, but I thought you said your name was Popof?"

"I did. Popof is Grushenkov—same thing."

"I see. And, if I might suggest, it would be better if you left word that you would be through in fifteen minutes. I know that Postumus has an appointment in that time."

"I am caring what Postumus has? I'm calling on Gallus."

"Sorry, sir, but Postumus is Gallus, you know."

"O. K.! Postumus, Gallus, Drusus—so long as I get in."

*   *   *   *   *

He enters the inner sanctum and the following greeting takes place:

"Hi, Galba!"

"Well, I'll be darned—Vasily!"

The natural outcome would be that the Russian's daughter marries the Roman's son, and they have a little boy named Vasily Caius Ivanovitch Gallus, Popof Drusus Tchitchorna Postumus Grushenkov, Galba, or "Jimmy," for short.

Eat
More Worry

AND now it turns out that we must worry! Worry is the new health fad. That much-maligned emotion has come into its own as a body-builder, along with yeast-eating, nudism and bending over twenty times to touch second base.

All this comes from a doctor of psychology, so it must come pretty straight. Doctors of psychology are the ones who have been telling us all along *not* to worry, so they certainly ought to know what's what in the worry racket.

"When we worry," says the doc, "every gland in the body pours energizing juices into the brain. It is the body's way of preparing the mind to meet an emergency. The biological purpose of worry is to enable you to get up steam."

*   *   *   *   *

Following are a set of worrying exercises for sluggish natures. Get those energizing juices to flowing!

148

*Lie flat on your back with your
legs in the air*

Position No. 1.—On arising stand facing an
open window. (Not too wide open, as, if you
get to worrying too well, you may fly out.)
Place the hands lightly on the hips and think:
"On the fifteenth that big insurance premium
comes due. On the fifteenth the income tax is
due. On the fifteenth I shall be just eight hundred dollars short of meeting them." Repeat
this ten times and then exhale.

Position No. 2.—Lie flat on your back, with
your legs in the air, and run over in your mind
the age at which you find yourself, the amount
of money you have saved, the probable number of years left, and what chances you will have
of getting a ten-year guest-card at the Home for
Aged Men. As soon as the energizing juices
have reached your feet lower them and adopt a
sitting posture on the floor. Sit that way all
day, with your chin in your hand.

Position No. 3.—Stand in front of a mirror and look at your stomach.

Position No. 4.—Wake yourself up in the middle of the night, lie flat on your back in bed and look at the ceiling. Then figure out just how you would get out of the house in case of fire, what you would do first if that pain in your side should turn out to be acute appendicitis, or how you would face an actual werewolf.

Position No. 5.—Just stop to think about *any-*thing.

* * * * *

If you will conscientiously follow these in-structions day by day, supplemented by our special worry-gland tablets, which are guaranteed to pour energizing juices into the brain, it will be no time at all before you are a new man, and one that you will not like.

Keep
a Log

IN PLANNING that automobile trip up-
country this Summer don't forget to consult
those notes you made last year when going over
the same route. They're in that combination
log-book and Japanese fan that you took along
for just that purpose.

These notes, most of which were jotted down
en route, seem to have been made with the
wrong end of the pencil. They are part lead-
markings and part wood-carvings. It would be
fun to dig up that pencil today, just to take a
look at it and see where the lead stopped and
the wood began.

To make things harder you apparently made
the notes while taking part in a hill-climbing
contest, when the car was at an angle of forty-
five degrees. They are the work of a man in
rather desperate straits to keep himself in his
seat, to say nothing of indulging in the luxury
of writing. You *couldn't* have been as drunk
as that.

*   *   *   *   *

The first one, jotted down with great difficulty, was made opposite the name of the town, East Mipford, fifteen miles from your starting place. It says, as nearly as you can make it out, simply "East Mipford." This would seem rather silly. Presumably you already knew the name of the town, as it was right there in the map in plain letters. Why jot it down again in that round, boyish hand of yours? Possibly you were just practicing handwriting. God knows you needed practice!

Anyway, there is "East Mipford" and, opposite it, "East Mipford," so East Mipford it is. It's a good thing to know, at any rate.

The next bit of puzzle work was jabbed into the paper at Orkington. Here you saw fit to write "No sporfut." Either this was meant as a warning that, at Orkington, one can get no "sporfut" or that it is dangerous to "sporfut" in or around, Orkington. If you had some clearer idea of what "sporfut" was you would know better how to regulate your passage through Orkington this year. The lack of "sporfut" last year must have been quite a trial to you, otherwise you wouldn't have made a note of it. Well, better luck this time!

*   *   *   *   *

At Animals' Falls you had what was designated as "lunch," which is pretty easy to figure out. After it, however is written "Gleever House—Central Hotel—Animals' Falls Spa." It must have been a pretty good "lunch" to have included all three restaurants, and, as you made no designation of which was best, the only thing to do is try them all again this time.

Perhaps you will remember, after ordering at the Gleever House, that it was the Central Hotel which was the best. Perhaps you meant that all three were rotten and that you should go on to the next town before eating. The only way to find out is to try.

From then on you are confronted by such notations as "fresh cob" at Turkville (which may mean "fresh cop" or good "fresh corn on the cob"), "Emily" at North Neswick (which may be where you left Emily off), and "steening chahl" at Lurding, which obviously means nothing. You arrived at your destination, according to the log, at "27 o'clock."

*　*　*　*　*

That is the value of a log-book. It makes the second trip seem so much more exciting.

Lost
Youth

JUST to show how things can go on under one's very nose without one's being aware of them, I find that I was in Worcester, Mass., when the first giraffe ever to be brought to the United States was shown first on the Worcester Common. And now is the first time I ever knew of it!

Now, a giraffe is not an animal that one sees for the first time without looking twice. A giraffe, no matter how you look at it, is out of the ordinary. And the first giraffe ever to be seen in the United States must have made more of an impression on Worcester Common than just an ordinary four-footed friend pattering along. Worcester isn't as blasé as all that.

Of course, I was only three years old at the time, but a child three years old has ears. I knew the words to *Ta-ra-ra-boom-de-ay*. I surely could have been trusted with the information that there was a giraffe down on the Common, especially when no one had ever seen a giraffe before.

* * * * *

154

I always knew that my father was a phlegmatic man, but I didn't realize that he was as phlegmatic as that. His office was in the City Hall, which backed right up on the Common, and from his window he certainly could have seen that something was up.

I can hardly believe that when he came home to dinner and my mother asked him: "What was the news downtown today?" he said: "Nothing much. Oh, yes, there was an animal out on the Common with a neck that reached up into the trees and all covered over with spots. A giraffe, I think they said. . . . What's for dinner tonight?"

Why wasn't I taken down to see it? I was taken to watch fireworks on the Fourth of July, and hated it. I was taken to the circus, and all that the circus had to offer was some old elephants and tigers that everybody had seen before. But they held out on me when a real attraction came to town. Maybe they thought it would be over my head, and so help me I didn't mean to write it that way. (However, you notice that I'm letting it stand.)

It is very lucky that I didn't happen to be out for a stroll by myself and discover that giraffe without any warning. Still, I suppose that, at the age of three, nothing surprises one.

But I'll bet that there was many a man in Worcester who went on the wagon for good in 1893.

*   *   *   *   *

The same news story that broke the news to me that I had missed the first giraffe in 1893, stated that the first elephant was brought to this country in 1796 by Captain Jacob Crowninshield, of Salem, Mass. (Massachusetts seems to have gone in for frightening folks.)

However little impression the first giraffe may have made on Worcester or my father, I wouldn't want to have been in Salem on the night when the first elephant put in an appearance. Three years old or not, I'll bet I should have remembered *that*!

The
Ice-Breaker

TODAY I heard a man say to his parrot: "Roll over!" and the parrot rolled over. This set me to thinking.

What would be the first thing you would do if you wanted to make a parrot roll over, short of rolling it over yourself? I can understand possibly teaching a parrot to speak, but how would you approach the problem of making it roll over?

Would you go right up to it and say: "Roll over!" and then wait? I don't quite see the common ground that one could get on with a parrot as a starter for such an experiment. There must be some initial move to be made and I am glad that I am not the one who has to make it.

It is these initial moves that get me down. What is the very first thing a man does when he sets out to build a bridge? How do you decide where to dig the first shovelful of earth in making a road? On the first day of work in erecting a skyscraper, what is the very first move made?

*　*　*　*　*

I could probably build a bridge or erect a skyscraper—or even teach a parrot to roll over—if someone would get the job started for me, but I know perfectly well that, if I were handling any one of these enterprises I would spend the first day gazing into space, trying to figure out how to begin. Fortunately, as yet, no one has come to me with a skyscraper to be erected or a bridge to be built, and, as I am in my middle forties now, it doesn't look as if anyone is going to.

Still, you can't ever tell. Joseph Conrad didn't begin to write until he was forty. Napoleon never even saw a steamboat until he was fifty-eight. Mozart never wrote a bar of music until he was ninety. Anything can happen, but it usually doesn't.

I am still worrying about that parrot. Did the parrot come to the man, maybe, and say: "Teach me to roll over!"? That, at least, would have broken the ice.

Oh, well, I've got better things to do than worry about breaking the ice with a parrot—but right now I can't think what they are.

The
Piano-Playing Record

A MR. JOHN STRICKLAND, of Black-pool, England, claims to have set a new world's record for consecutive hours of piano-playing. He played for 122½ hours without a stop. I haven't really checked yet, but I think that the woman in the next apartment to mine is worth grooming as a challenger. She has the spirit, all right, and it would only be a question of wind.

Posing as merely an interested observer and student of long-distance piano-playing, I have written Mr. Strickland, asking him a few questions. What I really had in mind was finding out his technique, so that I could steal its best features in a system of training for the woman in the next apartment. A rather dirty trick, but all's fair in love and, etc.

*   *   *   *   *

Here are the questions I asked him, together with his answers:

Q. What goes on in your mind during the 122½ hours?

A. I try not to think any more than I can help. That is a pretty long time for consecutive thinking. I more or less run over in my mind the main points of English history from the Norman Conquest to the Reform Act, and try to figure out how they would have been changed if Englishmen had all been colored. Then I go over the whole thing again, making believe that England was under water all of the time. This gets pretty fascinating along about the Wars of the Roses.

For relaxation I just sit and wonder what I'm doing at the piano, anyway. You see, I really wanted to be a marine architect.

Q. What tunes do you play?

A. I begin with *Chop Sticks* and run along with that for a day or two, shifting octaves every four hours. This gives quite a bit of variety. Then I go into *The Skaters* waltz, of which I know only the air and one chord of the bass. I find that popular music of the ballad type lends itself easily to repetition, as most of the songs are alike, and I have fun trying to figure out which one it is that I am playing.

Q. How do you take your meals?

A. How do you take *yours*?

Q. You needn't be so surly about it!

A. You mind your business, then!

Q. How do you handle complaints from neighbors?

A. I have no neighbors any more.

Q. Don't your hands get tired?

A. When they do I lean over and play with my chin. When that gets tired I play first with my right cheek and then with my left.

Q. What—no foot-work?

A. Now you are just being silly!

Q. How do you train for a long-distance exhibition?

A. For one like my 122½-hour record-breaker I run a trial-heat of 122½ hours, just to get the hang of the thing.

Q. Do you think that the whole thing is worth while?

A. There you have me!

*   *   *   *   *

Being a man of science, and understanding the spirit of my research, Mr. Strickland appends an anecdote of his early years of piano-playing when he was in school. There was a rule in the college which he attended forbidding "music between the hours of ten and one." In calling Mr. Strickland to task one day the dean wrote: "I am afraid that, for purposes of discipline, your piano-playing must be regarded as music."

I am forwarding Mr. Strickland's replies to my questionnaire to the lady in the next apartment. I hope that she will stop long enough to read it.

Fun
with Animals

THE news that a small, blackfoot penguin in the New York Aquarium had sprained its ankle when it stepped on a marshmallow served only to remind us that no one of God's creatures, however smart, is immune from loss of dignity. No one is infallible.

If anyone ought to be able to walk along without slipping, it is a penguin. Accustomed to treading the slippery surfaces of the globe with considerable assurance, if not manner, the penguin is one animal from whom you would expect accurate footwork.

And yet one small marshmallow, undoubtedly left there by an admirer, threw this penquin to the tune of a sprained ankle.

I worked on a motion picture once with a penguin named Eddie. Eddie put on quite a lot of airs for himself as a stroller, but I never saw him walk ten feet without tripping over a cable or something, and tripping rather badly, too. When Eddie tripped, he fell, and fell heavily, but he was always up again in a thrice, pretending that he had just been clowning.

There is a great satisfaction to us clumsy humans when we see an animal that is supposed to surpass us in skill making a monkey of itself.

*   *   *   *   *

I am still gloating over a blackbird that I saw, with my own eyes, in as disgraceful a bit of flying as any novice ever put on.

I was sitting in an automobile by the side of the curb when this bird swooped down. With some idea, evidently, of making a two-point landing, just to show off. Well, just as his feet hit the sidewalk, one of them slipped out from under him, and I was a witness to the remarkable sight of a full-grown, adult bird falling on its tail. A vaudeville comic couldn't have taken a neater spill.

The chagrin and humiliation of that blackbird were gratifying to see. He got back his balance immediately and tried to act as if nothing had happened, but he knew that I had seen him and he was furious. He was off in the air again right away, but not before I had sneered: "Nya-ya!" at him and called "Get a horse!"

Everyone ought to see a bird slip on its tail at least once. It is a gratifying experience and one good for the soul.

The Children's Hour

I DON'T want to be an alarmist, but I think that the Younger Generation is up to something. I think that there is a plot on foot.

I base my apprehension on nothing more definite than the fact that they are always coming in and going out of the house, without any apparent reason. When they are indoors, they sit for a while without doing anything much. Then they suddenly decide to go out again for a while. Then they come in again. In and out— in and out.

Of course, this applies only to Saturdays and vacation time. I don't know what they do at school but presumably they stay put. They can't just wander in and out of classrooms and school buildings as they do at home.

* * * * *

This foot-loose tendency is most noticeable during Spring and Summer vacations. Let us say that two or three of them leave the house right after breakfast. In answer to the question:

165

"Where are you going this morning?" they say: "Oh, just around."

In half an hour they are back, with possibly three others. They don't talk. They just come in. Sometimes they sit down in various attitudes of abandon. Sometimes they walk slowly around the room. Sometimes they just stand and lean against the wall. Then, after perhaps five minutes of this, they start outdoors again in a body.

This goes on all day. Each time they return, they have two or three new ones with them, but there seems to be no reason why fresh members have come. They don't act as if it made any difference to them *where* they were. They do not even appear to enjoy each other's company very much. They are very quiet about it all, except for slamming the screen door. It is ominous.

* * * * *

All that I can figure out is that they are plotting a revolution. When they go out, I think that they work secretly on laying cement foundations for gun-bases, or even lay mines. Then they come indoors to look around and see if the old folks have begun to suspect anything yet. Assuring themselves that all is well, someone gives the signal and they are off again to their plotting.

I don't think that anyone but mothers and fathers of adolescent families will know what I mean, but I have spoken to several parents about it and they have all noticed the same thing. There is a restlessness abroad among the Young Folk, but it is a quiet, shambling sort of restlessness which presages a sudden bugle call some day, at which they will all spring into action.

* * * * *

All that I ask is that they let me in on their plans. It would help if they were noisier about the thing and did a little yelling now and then. It's this constant coming in and going out of the house like slippered Moslems fomenting a revolt that gets me down.

All I hope is that they start something—anything—before I am too old to run.

Back
to Mozart

SOME time ago, in this space, I attempted to cheer up others, who felt Life closing in on them with nothing accomplished, by writing that Napoleon never saw a steamboat until he was fifty-eight and that Mozart never wrote a bar of music until he was ninety.

A very pleasant lady correspondent has written in to ask me if there has not been some mistake. She has always understood, she says, that Mozart died at the age of thirty-five and that he began to compose at the age of four.

I don't believe that we can be thinking of the same Mozart. The Mozart that I meant was Arthur Mozart, who lived at 138th street until he died, in 1926, at the age of ninety-three.

This Mozart that I referred to was a journeyman whistler, who went about from place to place, giving bird calls and just plain whistles. He was a short, dark man, with a mustache in which everyone claimed he carried a bird. After his death this was proven to be a canard. (This

is not a pun on the French word for "duck."
He didn't carry a duck there, either.)

*　　*　　*　　*　　*

Up until the age of ninety, however, Arthur
had never composed anything for himself to
whistle, always relying on the well-known bird
calls and popular airs of the day. That is, they
were popular until Arthur gave them a
workout.

But just before his ninetieth birthday, the
Mozarts got together and decided that
"Grampa Arthur," as they called him, ought
to unbelt with a little something for posterity.
So they gave him a pitch-pipe, and stood
around waiting for him to swallow it.

But, instead of swallowing it, Mozart went
into the next room and worked up a fairly hot
number for woodwinds and brasses, called
"Opus No. 1," because it was such hard work.
It was a steal from Debusset, but the cadenzas
were Mozart's. He also went into the coda right
after the first six bars.

This Arthur Mozart is the one I had refer-
ence to in my article. The Mozart that my correspondent refers to was evidently a prodigy of
some sort, if he composed at the age of four. He
also must have worked on one of the night-club

pianos like Harry Richman's. Maybe it was Harry Richman!

All this shows what comes of not giving initials when you mention a name in print. But how was I to know that there were two Mozarts who were composers?

Frog-Farming

A WARNING has gone out from the Conservation Commission against too sanguine investment in frog farms. I am one of the most warnable people alive, but I don't have to be told to look out for frog farms. I know about them.

Mr. MacGregor and I started a frog farm on a small scale only last year, but somehow we couldn't seem to make a go of it. I don't think that Mr. MacGregor used the right tactics with the frogs personally. Having been in the Navy during the War he was accustomed to being obeyed. You can't yell "Avast!" at a frog and expect it to avast, or even to stand at attention. MacGregor was too gruff with them.

Possibly we didn't have the right sort of corral for them. We used the next room. It was nice and light in the next room, and we had pans of water and dog biscuit around everywhere but they didn't seem happy. They never moved around much except when Mr. MacGregor went in to take care of them.

*　*　*　*　*

The first day that we had the frog farm, Mac-Gregor put on a pair of overalls and went in to do the chores. In a minute he came out, dis-spirited:

"I can't make them hold still," he said, in a hurt tone.

"What do you want them to hold still for?" I asked, trying to get at the bottom of the trouble quietly, instead of flying into a panic right at the start.

"How are you going to bathe a frog if it won't hold still?" he asked. "Just as I get squatted down, it hops half way across the room."

"Maybe you ought to set it up on a table in front of you," I suggested. "Then you wouldn't have to squat down. I'd jump half way across the room myself if you squatted down beside me."

"No danger of that," he said testily. "You think it's fun to chase a frog all around a room with a stool. Here you sit in this room, 'taking care of the books,' as you say ——"

*   *   *   *   *

"Somebody's got to take care of the books if we're going to run a farm scientifically," I re-

172

plied. "Modern farming isn't the haphazard thing it was when you were a boy, you know."

"Well, supposing I take care of the books for a while and you do the chores." MacGregor was getting sullen. "What have you got to put in the books, anyway? We haven't made a sale yet."

"I'm working up a bill head," I replied very calmly. And I showed him a nicely lettered bill head reading:

MacGregor & Benchley
FINE FROGS

"Is that all you're going to say—just *Fine Frogs?*" he asked.

"What do you want to say—*Fine Frogs, You Bet,* or *Fine Frogs for Fussy Folk?*" There was a note of exasperation in my voice.

"I mean *what kind* of fine frogs? What are they for—fighting, breeding, steeplechasing ——?"

*   *   *   *   *

This brought up a question which we hadn't thought of before—just what were our frogs going to be sold for? We couldn't hope to get along on just the frogs' legs market, and practically no one has a frog as a pet these days.

"Let's go into the stables and see what they

do best," I suggested. "Take off your overalls and put on your puttees, and we'll take a look at the stock."

On arriving in the next room, however, our problem was solved for us. There were no frogs at all. We looked under the chairs and the filing cabinet, and even out the window, but the frogs had gone. Our bubble had burst.

So we dissolved partnership and went out of business. But we still keep the next room shut off—just in case.

My
Orchard

I USED to think that I was fairly adaptable to any unfamiliar circumstances in which I might find myself. Give me ten or fifteen minutes to get fully awake and I could make the best of a jail cell in Port Said or the Center Court at Wimbledon. I say the "best," I mean *my* best.

But I cannot believe that I am even making my best out of the present situation. I find myself the lessee of several orange, lemon and tangerine trees, which grow in the back yard of a house that I have rented, and adaptable as I am, I cannot seem to get the swing of it.

I have had gardens before, but they were vegetable gardens, where things grew in and on the ground—when they grew at all. But these things are up above my head, and they belong to *me* —for a few months. I might as well have been given the use of a captive balloon.

I go out into the yard and look up at them from one side, and then walk around and look up at them from the other side. Then I walk back into the house. This has been going on for days.

*　　*　　*　　*　　*

As I stand looking at them I realize that they are oranges and lemons all right. I have seen oranges and lemons growing before. But these are *my* oranges and lemons. And they are up so high. It is an impossible situation.

I suppose that I could pick some of them, but that would be a violation of something, I don't know what. When I need oranges and lemons I will buy them through the recognized channels. No lease in the world could possibly make it legitimate for me to break off one of those stems. It is probably a throw-back to the days when I used to get chased for robbing pear trees.

So every day I go out and look up at my oranges and lemons. Then, overcome with the futility of anything so tangible and so high off the ground belonging to me, I walk back into the house again. Oddly enough, these little excursions into my orchard throw me off balance for the rest of the day. I don't know where I stand about *any*thing.

*　　*　　*　　*　　*

Unfortunately, I am living alone at the time,

and so have no one to confide in. If there were only some one to come out with me and say: "They aren't yours, anyway. They really belong to the people who own the house," then I would be relieved.

As it stands, I am in a rather serious state of maladjustment.

Hedgehogs Wanted

A N ADVERTISEMENT in a London paper reads: "5,000 Hedgehogs Wanted." Of course, it's none of my business, especially as it is an Englishman that wants them, but I trust that I may speculate to myself without giving offense.

One hedgehog I could understand, or possibly two, to keep each other company. There is no accounting for taste in pets, and I suppose you could get as attached to a hedgehog as you could to a dog, if you went about it in the right way. I, personally, would prefer a dog, but then, I'm dog-crazy.

But 5,000 hedgehogs seem to be overdoing it a bit. When you get up into the thousands with hedgehogs you are just being silly, it seems to me. And, aside from the looks of the thing, there is the very practical angle that you might very well find yourself hedgehog-poor.

* * * * *

There must be something that hedgehogs do

that I don't know about that makes them desirable to have around in large numbers. They may keep away flies, or eat moths, or even just spread out in a phalanx and prevent workmen from lying down on the ground, or picnic parties from camping out on private property. Whatever their special function, it must be preventive.

Of course, there may be something in the back of the man's mind about quills. He may be forming a gigantic toothpick combine or starting a movement back to the old quill pen. In this case, he has his work cut out for him. Shearing, or plucking, or shaving 5,000 hedgehogs is going to be no sinecure. And he is going to run out of swear-words the first day. Just the plain, ordinary "ouch" is going to get him nowhere.

On the whole, my advice would be to give the whole project up, whatever it is. Unless, of course, the advertisement has been answered already and he has his 5,000 hedgehogs on his hands. In that case, I don't know *what* to advise.

Skol!

PROFESSOR KLAUS HANSEN, of Norway, has announced that he recently drank a 98 per cent solution of "heavy water" (H O) without experiencing any ill effects. That's what he thinks. That's what the man said who first drank an Alexander cocktail (one-half gin, one-quarter creme de Cacao, one-quarter sweet cream).

The professor admitted that he had "to fight against hysteria" when he saw a mouse that drank heavy water at the same time show signs of illness immediately after the experiment. The mouse was no fool, obviously. He didn't even have to fight against hysteria.

* * * * *

Of course, I would have to fight against hysteria if I simply saw a mouse. Following a drink of heavy water, or even vodka, the presence of a mouse in the room would give me the tip-off. Next would come the muskrats, then the mongeese, and then, in sly succession, the larger, more vivid animals. When one is experimenting with a new drink the fewer livestock there are around the better.

However, there is one item in the cable from Norway which makes me think that Professor Hansen may have hit on something. It is in the form of a follow-up, and it reads:

"Professor Klaus Hansen, of Oslo University, was so pleased today with his first quaff of heavy water that he ordered two litres (2.1134 quarts) more, valued at 20,000 kroner (about $5,080), for further experiments."

Now, in the first place, that runs into money. You don't order drinks "for further experiments" at $2,000 a throw unless there are certain pleasing features connected with it. It says that "Professor Hansen was so pleased," which is probably the scientific way of saying that "Professor Hansen was still cockeyed."

Of course, someone else is paying the check, but, even at that, there is a lordly, free-handed air about the ordering that indicates that heavy water is not a depressant, at any rate.

And what about the mouse? Does he get in on the "future experiments," or does he go back on scotch and plain water, just because he got a little sick on his first drink? He took just the same chance that the professor did. He may not have held it so well, but, if it is as good as it seems to be, he certainly ought to be given another whack at it. Maybe he just drank his first one too fast. He was just a kid.

*   *   *   *   *

Until the price comes down it doesn't look as if many of us will get a chance to see what there is in heavy water that "pleased" Professor Hansen so. The formula is simple—just two parts more hydrogen than there is in ordinary water.

We might be able to whip up a tubful in the kitchen some time and give it a try, with a little orange bitters. I don't suppose that it would stand much shaking. That hydrogen is tricky stuff.

*   *   *   *   *

On the whole, it might be better to wait for the reports on the professor's next session with it. He may think now that he wants some more, but, when the time comes and he gets the glass to his lips, he may string right along with the mouse.

Often one *thinks* that one has had a good time with some new drink, but when the showdown comes for a repeat a slight repulsion sets in, and one realizes that the good time came from the singing or the company. Drinks get an awful lot of credit in retrospect that they don't deserve.

However, here's to Professor Hansen for taking the chance, and here's to the University of Oslo for being such a charming host to the tune of 20,000 kroner! And here, also, is to the mouse!

Comes
the Eclipse

I DON'T want to be an alarmist, but there is going to be a total eclipse of the moon at 11:09 P. M. on July 15th, visible from all cars. The time is Eastern Standard. The moon is that same old yellow thing.

There is also going to be a partial eclipse of the sun on July 30th, but it will be invisible in the United States, so go right ahead with whatever you are doing at the time. You can look, if you want to, but you will hurt your eyes.

* * * * *

On the night of July 15th, at 11:09 P. M., I am planning to have quite a time, if I can manage to stay up that late and get out-of-doors. That getting out-of-doors is going to be the tough part. At 11:09 P. M. things are just beginning to get good indoors.

But it seems to me that here will be a chance to do a lot of things that I have wanted to do, but have been held back from by fear of publicity. I have arranged a little schedule, beginning at 10:12 P. M., when the eclipse begins, and ending at 1:47 A. M., when the eclipse ends.

At 10:12 I will put on my white suit, which I don't seem able to wear in the daytime without blushing, and go out into the garden.

Once in the garden I will pick some flowers. I have had a little hesitancy about picking flowers in the garden in the daytime, or moonlight, because I don't know quite what the procedure is. Do you lurch heavily into the flowers until they break off or do you shoot them off with an air rifle? At 10:15 on that night I shall get them off somehow and I don't want anyone to peek.

*   *   *   *   *

As the eclipse progresses I am going to start a gramophone and waltz. I have always wanted to waltz, but there has always been too much light. I think that I might be very good, but, on the other hand, I might be a disappointment. I will try it without a partner at first, and then if I think that it is going well I may send for a local girl to come in by the hour.

I think that then I will get my rowing machine out from under my bed and take it into the garden and row on it. I have had that rowing machine now for three years and have never been able to bring myself to work it, for fear that a son or somebody might come in and see me. When the eclipse is at its darkest I shall start rowing. I may not get much exercise in that short time, but at least, I shall have used the machine once.

There are several books I want to read and faces I want to make in those minutes between 10:12 P. M. and 1:47 A. M., and I might even knit a little.

All in all it looks like a big night for me.

Autographs for Sale

A COPY of *The Autograph Review* which has just come to hand (having evidently been in my pocket since 1930, as that is the date on it) presents a slightly more dignified side of the current scramble for autographs than we get from those little brown people who infest the entrances to theatrical and motion picture premières.

In *The Autograph Review* are listed some of the choice items which may be had by sending a nominal sum to the editor. For instance:

Item No. 1—SHAW, GEORGE BERNARD. Fine short A. L. S. (Autograph Letter Signed), one page, on card of Holyhead Hotel, March 28, 1913. To Maurice Bourgeois. Shaw writes that he is on his way to Ireland for an Easter vacation and that his movements are very uncertain and undecided. Signed in full. .$25.00

Item No. 8—HOUSMAN, LAURENCE. Singular A. L. S. in which Housman demonstrates his mania for self-effacement. He explains that he broke with John Lane, the pub-

lisher, because Lane used his photograph for purposes of journalistic advertising. A most curious letter $13.50
Item No. 9—LARCOM, LUCY. Original A. MSS. S. of her poem, *What Is It?* One very full page, oblong quarto. The poem contains forty lines $9.00
And so it goes, on through fifty items, ranging an impressiveness from a $50 Oscar Wilde to a collection of eight signatures, including Benjamin F. Butler, Henry Wilson and W. A. Buckingham, for seventy-five cents. The paper alone is worth that.

* * * * *

I, too, have a collection of signatures which I will gladly turn over to the editor of *The Autograph Review*, or will sell direct from this office. The prices listed are subject to indefinite wrangling.
Item No. 1—McGRATH, LUCIUS G. Deputy Sheriff in Westchester County. Short A. L. S., one page. To the editor of this column. McGrath states that he has been through the files and can find no record of my ever having paid that $9.82 fine on my 1932 State income tax. He gives an indication that he has the next step in mind. Very interesting........$0.11

Item No. 2—STEWART, DONALD OGDEN. An especially curious cheque for $3.50, returned from the Bankers' Trust Company for verification of signature. The "O" in the name "Ogden" has four concentric circles in connection with it, as if the writer had got going and couldn't stop. A valuable item for collectors of unusual letter "O's"..................$3.40

Item No. 3—ROOSEVELT, PHILIP J. Short A. L. S. written to editor of this column. In his more formal manner, Roosevelt suggests payment of annual dues to Signet Society of Harvard University, as of June, 1911. Very old $0.10

* * * * *

Item No. 4—IMBRIE, LESTER W. Long, closely-written A. L. S. on ruled paper, in pencil. In it, Imbrie implies that he is at present being shadowed by agents of the Hapsburgs with the idea of seizing him and putting him on the throne of Austria. He says that he does not want to be put on the throne of Austria, as he gave up all that sort of thing when he abdicated in 1840 to take up active work in the "Kingdom Come" movement. He feels that he is just on the verge of success in bringing about the Day of Judgment and doesn't want to be taken off the job at this crucial moment. He suggests that the editor of this column do something about it, or, at any rate, get in touch with the Hapsburgs. From then on the meaning is not quite clear. Odd example of Spencerian penmanship .... Cartage charges

Item No. 5—MANUSCRIPT. First draft of present article with author's corrections and large ginger ale blister.... Price optional with purchaser

Health
and Work

A RATHER horrible bit of news has just come to this desk. We are informed that the eminent surgeon Dr. G. W. Crile has gone on record as saying that "with proper attention to health a person's active life in business should extend to the age of eighty years." What is this man Crile—an alarmist?

In the first place, how can a person give "proper attention to health" and still remain in "active life in business"? It is hard enough just to remain in active business without monkeying around with your health. "Let well enough alone" would be my advice to anyone with an active business.

Furthermore, what is so tantalizing about the idea of staying in active business life until the age of eighty? I know that there are supposed to be veterans who simply have to patter down to the office or the foundry every day, just out of sheer love of the thing, but they must also have some other reason for their devotion to work. There must be someone at home who gets on their nerves.

* * * * *

Anyone who has given what Dr. Crile calls "proper attention to health" should, by the age of fifty, be so sick of his work that he can't even glance through the trade papers without gagging. Any further exertion on his part is either because of necessity or is just sheer affectation.

Don Herold once wrote some *obiter dicta,* in the course of a book on something else, which have always been a great comfort to me. At the bottom of a page, in small italic type apparently dropped there by the printer, he said simply: "Work is a form of nervousness." It had no connection with the rest of the page, but it might have been made into a book by itself.

Mr. Herold is the man who also wrote that during the trying period when his young daughter was having her teeth straightened her mouth looked like the back of a telephone switchboard. This, together with his epic exposé of work, qualifies him, in my mind, for the position of the Moses of our generation.

* * * * *

"Work is a form of nervousness." Just think that over. It has the wisdom of the ages in it. And then think of Dr. Crile's threat that, with proper attention to health, a man can still be active in business at eighty. How are the other people in the office going to like having a nervous octogenarian lunging about the place?

The thing to do is to make so much money that you don't have to work after the age of twenty-seven. In case this is impracticable, stop work at the earliest possible moment, even if it is at a quarter past eleven on the morning of the day when you find you do have enough money. Then will be time enough to pay proper attention to your health. What is the sense of being in good health if you have to work?

Experience
Meeting

ONE of these days I have got to go and see a doctor about my cigarette smoking. I am slowly but surely losing the knack.

The thing has crept up on me insidiously. I didn't realize that I was smoking fewer and fewer cigarettes each day until I found that I had been carrying around an unopened pack in my pocket for three weeks. That sort of thing gets one after a while, you know.

I started out all right. I began, in the customary manner, with cubebs and bamboo. (When you broke the bamboo you found blood from your tongue in it. Hot dog!) Then sweet fern, dried leaves and, finally, a real cigarette! I was a regular boy, all right!

*   *   *   *   *

For quite a while I carried on, and seemed to be well set in the cigarette habit. I even had a favorite brand, although, as I look back on it now, I realize that I wasn't what you would call a slave to it. Another brand substituted in my

194

There was something about lighting a
cigarette that gave one a debonair look

mouth while I was day-dreaming and I wouldn't
have known the difference.

Then I began to find myself lighting cigarettes and putting them down on ash trays and
forgetting them. There was something about
lighting a cigarette that gave one a debonair
look, but once I had looked debonair I was
through for the day.

But after a few days I found myself stopping even that. I carried cigarettes about with me; admirers from all over the world gave me cigarette cases which I constantly left on my bureau, and I gave all the indications of being a cigarette smoker, except that I didn't smoke the cigarette.

One of the things that has contributed to my present condition is, I think, my inability to typewrite, or do anything else, with a cigarette in my mouth. I see other boys working away with a fag hanging from the corners of their lips, but, when I try it, the smoke gets up my nose and into my eyes and I can't see the paper. Even smoke from a cigarette which is lying in an ash tray has a way of seeking out my nose, no matter which way the wind is blowing. Maybe it's my nose that's at fault.

Whatever the reason, I now realize, too late, that I am a confirmed non-cigarette smoker.

* * * * *

Possibly if the cigarette companies would change their advertising I might reform. If they should say: "Bamboos Are Definitely Injurious to the Health," or "Smokes Wear You Down to a Nub," or "Light a Blazer and Shorten Your Life," then I might take the habit up again. All my other habits have proven disastrous through the centuries. Possibly all that I need is a little encouragement.

Child-Holding

FATHERS, god-fathers and uncles will be glad to learn that baby specialists have now decided that the child is given beneficial exercise by being shifted about from one position to another in the holder's arms. This will eliminate a great many dirty looks and much kidding at the male relative's expense.

No male relative, in his right mind, ever takes a baby to hold of his own free will. The very thought of dropping it, a thought which is always present, is enough to reduce all his vital organs to gelatin. Some female always suggests it. "Let Joe hold him for a minute. Hold him, Joe!"

So, Joe, sweating profusely, picks the infant up and becomes a figure of fun. "Look at how Joe's holding him, Bessie! Like he was a golf bag!" "Poor kid—put him down, Joe!" "Look out, Joe—you'll strangle him!" Lynching is on in the air.

* * * * *

But now Joe can come back with the excuse that he is giving the baby exercise. "You

*So Joe, sweating
profusely, becomes
a figure of fun*

women hold him in that one position all the
time, and his body doesn't develop symmetri-
cally. Ask any one who knows!"

For male relatives who find it necessary for
one reason or another to hold a baby, the following positions are suggested as being most
beneficial to the child's development and most
conducive of apprehension on the mother's part.

If the child has to be lifted from its crib by
the father or uncle, the old-fashioned way of
reaching down and grabbing it under the arms
should be discarded. The male relative should

get into the crib with the child, and lie on his back (his own back), taking the child on his chest and rising to a sitting posture. Then call for someone else to come and lift both father and child from the crib at once.

* * * * *

In taking the baby from the arms of someone else, as at the christening or general family gathering, grasp one of the child's ankles firmly in the right hand and tell the other person to let go. The child will then swing, head down, from the other person's arms, and can be twirled in a semi-circle, in the manner of an adagio dancer, until the arc is completed, and the child lands across the uncle's shoulder, the latter, if possible, still holding firmly onto the ankle. This will develop the child's leg, and give it poise.

For just ordinary holding, a good bit of exercise can be worked into a method whereby the male relative holds the child by both wrists and lets it hang down in front of him, swinging slowly back and forth like a pendulum. It can then be tossed high into the air and caught, or not, as Fate will have it.

A still better way to develop the child is to have *it* hold the male relative.

Rule
of Thumb

A LOT of us who were brought up on rhymes to aid us in memorizing academic rules and guides to living, find, as the years go by, that we are stuck with a lot of jingles with the key word missing. This can cause a lot of trouble.

I remember perfectly that "thirty days hath September, April, June and ——," but whether it is "November" or "December" is a mystery to me, and, although I have never been in a position where an extra day in a month, or an extra month in the year, made much difference one way or the other, I don't like to be in the dark like that.

I am letter perfect, except for one detail, on the old mariner's maxim: "—— skies at night, sailors' delight; —— skies in the morning, sailors take warning." All that I *don't* remember is what color sky it is—blue, red or gray. Fortunately, I gave up my early idea of going to sea, otherwise all my clients might have ended up on the rocks and reeking of seaweed, especially as my only other nautical rule is "Mackerel skies and mares' tails make good sailors —— —— their sails." The nub of this advice is whether to "pull down" or "put up" their sails. That one point eludes me.

*　　*　　*　　*　　*

In spelling, I need every aid to memory that man can devise and even then I can whip up a few novelties by myself. I am more the inspirational type of speller. I work on hunches rather than mere facts, and the result is sometimes open to criticism by purists.

So it really is a matter for serious pause on my part when I remember "*i* before *e*, except after —" and am then confronted with *c, d, e, g, p, t* and *v* as possible rhymes. Also, I am not even sure whether it is "*i* before *e*" or "*i* after *e*." This practically vitiates the rule as a guide to spelling, whatever virtues it may have as a jingle.

In the study of foreign languages, I am equipped with several rhythmic grammatical rules which mean nothing, because I have forgotten the pay-off. In German, I can swing along on *aus, ausser, bei, mit, nach, seit, von* and *zu,* and I know that these words all are followed by the same case. But is it dative or accusative? That's what I can't remember!

In Latin (which, fortunately, I am not called upon to use in my work-a-day routine) I can recite *ad, ante, con, in, post, prae, pro, sub* and *super*, but, if you ask me whether it is the accusative, ablative, gerundive or putative case that follows them, I blush prettily and say, "See my lawyer!" You can't expect a man to remember *every*thing!

* * * * *

In the matter of drinking (which, thank Heaven, I do not have to worry about, now that we have repeal!) there are several rhymes which can cause quite a bit of trouble.

Beer before wine,
Everything fine!

is all right as a slogan, unless you happen to think that it might be: "Beer *after* wine."

There is a world of difference there, my hearties! Ask any stomach specialist!

The trouble with rhymed rules is that the important words don't rhyme. The whole thing has got to be done over again, I'm afraid.

Quick Quotations

THE surest way to make a monkey of a man is to quote him. That remark in itself wouldn't make any sense if quoted as it stands.

The average man ought to be allowed a quotation of no less than three sentences, one to make his statement and two to explain what he meant. Ralph Waldo Emerson was about the only one who could stand having his utterances broken up into sentence quotations, and every once in a while even he doesn't sound so sensible in short snatches.

* * * * *

Take *par* (for) *example,* one of those newspaper columns of "Quotations of the Week," which has just dropped onto my desk, after a three-hour hunt for it on my part.

Granted that some of them wouldn't stack up very high even if they were quoted in full, they can't *all* be as fatuous as they sound:

"What the world needs more than anything

else is a revolution—but it must be a revolution of love."—*General Evangeline Booth.*

"Sex to me is something very high. It is a divine thing, and it is romantic, and that is the way I feel about it. And I think that is what I mean to the public. Allure, in a high way, because that is the manner in which I have portrayed it."—*Mae Murray.*

(Miss Murray got four sentences and still didn't quite do herself justice—or maybe she did.)

"Life does not come all in one piece like cheese; it more resembles linked sausages, a series of events on a string."—*Harold Bell Wright.*

(One has a horrible suspicion that Mr. Wright's remark really ended with that.)

"When you come right down to it, perhaps there are other things in life besides sex."—*Professor R. P. Sears.*

(One can be equally sure that Professor Sears was pretty sore when he saw just that one sentence quoted. It probably was part of a sly dig.)

"I'm really mentally lazy. I have to drive myself to write. But there's something inside that keeps nagging me to go on."—*Mary Pickford.*

*   *   *   *   *

Probably each one of these people, if confronted with the quotation, would say: "Well, yes, I did say that, but I didn't mean it the way it sounds. What I meant was ——"

So sure-fire is the fatuousness inherent in the average single-sentence quotation that several humorous publications have columns headed "You're Telling Us," in which embarrassed public characters may read their own remarks used as fun-fodder. A remark like: "I can't take a nap in the middle of the day," with Mr. Justice Hughes' name after it, would look pretty silly all by itself.

The best way to do, if you are one of those unfortunate people who are likely to be quoted in print, is to say everything you have to say in one long, periodic sentence, so that it can't be broken up.

Or, better yet, say nothing at all. (Don't quote me as having said that.)

Spy
Scares

WHENEVER you read about the unearth-
ing of a big international spy ring in
some European country, you may be pretty sure
that the government of that country has been
naughty and is trying to give the people something else to think about for a minute or two.

"O-o-oh! Look over there!" the government
is saying. "See dat dreat bid spy!" And, while
the public is looking, it tries to cram a bunch
of incriminating letters and contracts down the
drain pipe. It's an old gag, but a good one.

Of course, every government has spies in
every other country, and every other country
knows about them. It is merely a form of international courtesy, like exchange professors. So
long as the spies don't actually block traffic or
blow up the newer buildings, they can snap
their cameras and rattle their blueprints to
their hearts' content. In fact, they give a rather
nice cosmopolitan air to the streets.

*   *   *   *   *

207

*They give a rather nice cosmopolitan air
to the streets*

Now, if a government can get out of a jam
simply by crying "Spy-ring! Spy-ring!" why
can't individuals work the same strategy? There
must be some spies in your own neighborhood
that you could use in a pinch.

Let us say that you are due home for dinner
at seven. What with one thing and that other
thing, you are delayed until possibly one-thirty
in the morning, just too late for the roast lamb.
You don't want any dessert.

"What did you think we were having tonight
—a watch night service?" says the Little Woman,
barely opening her mouth to say it.

Don't you say a word. Just look serious.

"I suppose they were rebuilding the office and you got walled up in the masonry," she continues. "You were lucky to get out at all, I suppose."

* * * * *

Now is the time. "This is not the occasion for flippancy," you say. "Our country, your country and my country, is in peril."

This is a new one, and it has her stopped for a minute.

"What do you know about your friend Mrs. Geefer?" you continue, taking out your notebook and pencil.

"I know that she thinks that a two-spades bid means that she is to pass," comes the answer, without thinking. Then the eyes narrow. "What's this Mrs. Geefer element being injected into the conversation? What has she got to do with a half-past one dinner?"

"Mrs. Geefer is right now being kept under surveillance as a member of an international spy-ring. She, and a man named Wilcensic, are agents for the Soviet government."

"What did they do—make you head of the Secret Service? Is that what kept you so late?"

"We won't discuss my part in this affair. I am under sealed orders. The question is—do you care enough about your country's welfare to co-operate in tracking down this spy-ring?"

"You can go out into the kitchen and track down a coffee ring if you want something to eat; that's what *you* can track down. Or did they have food, too, at that brewers' track meet you were at?"

*　　*　　*　　*　　*

Things can go on like this until breakfast time or you can go out and make believe round up Mrs. Geefer yourself for your country. But the chances are that you will get nowhere with your spy scare. You have to have a bigger territory to work in.

That's one of the advantages of being a government instead of just a private liar.

Mistaken Notions

IF THERE is one thing that I resent (and there is), it is to be told that I resent being told anything. It drives me crazy.

I can take criticism and suggestions as well as anybody. In fact, the wonder is that I keep my head as well as I do, with all the criticism and suggestions that I get. But, frankly, I have just lost my temper and pretty badly, too. I have been told that I am "misinformed."

Somebody in a Sunday paper has got together a list of "mistaken notions," or things which ignorant people believe to be true, but which, according to this upstart, have no basis in fact at all. I find that I myself believe practically every one of them, which makes it more or less of an affair of honor between the author of the article and me.

*　　*　　*　　*　　*

His article is entitled: "How Badly Misinformed Are You About These Things?" The very tone of the title itself is offensive. "Misinformed," indeed! I think that I am the best judge of whether I am misinformed or not, and I'll take no back talk out of a Sunday feature writer.

The first point on which I am supposed to be "misinformed" is my belief that shaving makes hair grow faster. Well, Mr. Feature-writer, I happen to *know* that it does. He says that experiments have proved that it doesn't. And I ask you to read what his so-called "experiments" consists of:

"Any skeptic," he says, making a deliberate crack at me, "can test this easily by letting his whiskers grow for a year, cutting them off and weighing them, and then comparing this weight with the weight of bits of whisker shaved off every day for another year and carefully washed and saved."

In the first place, what does he mean by an "easy" test? Washing, saving and weighing whiskers over a period of two years wouldn't leave much time for anything else, although a man who would set out to wash, save and weigh his whiskers would probably not have much of anything else to do with his time. Certainly nobody would employ such a man on any other kind of job. Nobody would want to have him even around the house.

In the second place, I happen to *know* that shaving does make hair grow faster, so Mr. Smart Alec can just wash, save and weigh his own whiskers and see if it makes any difference to me in my belief.

* * * * *

Another thing on which I am supposed to be "misinformed" is my belief that rainy weather is the cause of rheumatism and rheumatic pains. I don't know about its being the cause exactly, but I just wish that the author of that piece could have my knee on a good damp day. I wish that he could have it on *any* day, as a matter of fact, but I don't necessarily want to take his knee in exchange.

I'll bet he has an awful knee. I'll bet that he is a very disagreeable person to live with, constantly going about and saying: "You're misinformed—you're misinformed."

I am furthermore told not to believe that pin pricks with a brass pin are poisonous, that night air is injurious to sick people, that lightning never strikes twice in the same place, that dishonest people usually have a narrow space between their eyes and that fright to a mother before a baby is born is liable to mark the child in some way.

*　　*　　*　　*　　*

All right, I may believe these things and I may not, but from now on they are a part of my credo. I'll take no dictation from some whippersnapper on a newspaper. "Misinformed," am I? I'll misinform *him*.

Maxims
from the Chinese

THREE crows are there, if only there were three crows. . . . Oh, well, anyway——!

* * * * *

The wise man moves fast, yet a great many times it is hard to catch him. This is because he has no soul. This is because he lives up there with all those radicals.

* * * * *

It is rather to be chosen than great riches, unless I have omitted something from the quotation.

* * * * *

One day Lee Fee was walking along the countryside, with his hands on his elbows. He was thinking, thinking, thinking. So far he has failed to interest us as a character.

"I am wondering," said Lee Fee aloud, in case anyone was asking him. "I am wondering what comes after 'W.'" And, as he wondered,

Lee Fee walked, and, as he walked, he wondered, and pretty soon he didn't know *what* he was doing.

Soon he came to Lee Fee, walking in the opposite direction. This put a stop to his monkey-business. He was good and scared. But he said: "Well, easy come, easy go!" and tried to brush by himself. But that is no easier than it seems.

"We are getting nowhere," said the east-bound Lee Fee to the west-bound Lee Fee. "Let's see if we can't come to some compromise. We are both sensible men, and there is a saying of Confucius that the sensible man goes but a short distance with himself before taking his own temperature. It is also said that eggs do not roll sideways. There is also an old saying ——"

But when Lee Fee looked up, Lee Fee was gone. He just couldn't take it. Too much wisdom gets on the wise man's nerves.

* * * * *

It is often difficult to tell whether a maxim means something, or something means maxim.

* * * * *

Three women were keeping house. It was too rainy. The First Old Woman said: "What wouldn't I give for three wishes at this very minute!"

"Well, what *wouldn't* you give?" asked the Second Old Woman.

"I wouldn't give my new silk coat, and I wouldn't give the roast pigeon in my oven, and I wouldn't give *that,*" replied the First Old Woman, snapping her fingers.

"And why wouldn't you give any of these things for three wishes?" asked the Third Old Lady, who had heard nothing of what was going on.

"Because, even if I had three wishes," replied the First Old Woman, dying, "what chance would there be of their being granted?"

A wish without the giver is bare.

* * * * *

The wise man thinks once before he speaks twice.

Excelsior!

I HAVE never really given the matter much thought," said Mr. MacGregor. (I had asked him how he would like to climb the Matterhorn.)

"Well, here we are in Switzerland on business," I said, "and there's the Matterhorn. What are you doing—day-dreaming?"

He opened his eyes very wide. "Who—me?" he asked.

Sometimes it is very difficult to hold MacGregor's attention. It isn't that he is not interested, but he doesn't seem to be able to express it. Some slip-shod habit of mind carried over from the Navy, I suppose.

"It looks like a set-up for you," I said. "Lots of people risk their lives every year climbing the Matterhorn, and there you sit, like a bump on a log. It ought to be your dish."

* * * * *

"Climbing mountains never interested me very much," said MacGregor, opening and shutting his watchcase.

"That's a very sub-thyroid attitude of mind,"

218

I said. "It's people like you who don't climb mountains."

"I guess you're right," he replied, sadly. "But I was always interested in Burton Holmes and his capers."

"There—you see?" I said, a little more harshly than I meant to. "You started out in—where was it?"

"Malden, Massachusetts," said MacGregor filling in an embarrassing pause.

"You started out in Malden, Massachusetts, with a definite interest in Burton Holmes. Then you got soft. You let liquor get the upper hand, and you thought it was smart to be a dilettante. If you had one ounce of stamina in you—to say nothing of consideration for our business—you would be up there on that mountain this minute, claiming it for the United States."

"Somebody owns it already, don't they?" asked MacGregor, in perfectly horrible English.

"If it isn't one excuse it's another," I said, going back to my paper. "Do as you like about it. I've had my say. I've done all any friend could do. You are your own worst enemy."

* * * * *

From where I sit writing I can see the Matterhorn, snow-capped, although it is only January. And, as I raise my binoculars to my eyes, I can discern a little figure trudging up the side of an enormous crag—the wrong crag, by the way, if one wishes to get to the top of the mountain.

But, anyway, MacGregor has won his fight with himself.

The
Rule of 87

THE trouble with modern civilization is that we have too many rules. Take, for example, what is known as "the Rule of 87" recently dragged out at the birth of quintuplets in Ontario and of (pardon me if I ask to see the data) sextuplets in Inotest, Rumania.

The Rule of 87, doubtless the work of fanatical reformers, is as follows: "One twin birth occurs to approximately 87 single births; one triplet to about 7,569 singles (87 squared) ; one quadruplet to about 658,503 singles (87 cubed) ; one quintuplet to about 57 million singles (87 to fourth power) ; one sextuplet to about five billion singles° (87 to fifth power) ."

That's the rule. That's what we are supposed to abide by, whether we want to or not. By whose authority was the "Rule of 87" promulgated! I should like to know. Probably, it was put over while the boys were away at war.

*   *   *   *   *

How long are we to stand for this arbitrary

rule that a man can't be the father of quintuplets until 57 million other people have had
one baby each? Is this Russia, or Germany we
are living in? Are we mice or are we men?

One of the sad features of this bondage to
statisticians is that it takes the heart out of an
ordinary man. What's the sense in going ahead,
if the figures are against you, if you are stymied
by a "Rule of 87"? Where does initiative come
in?

Remember Frank Tinney, who was afraid
to have a fourth child because he had heard
that every fourth child in the world was a
Chinaman. Is that any way to get new members?

*   *   *   *   *

I would not be one to set myself against constituted authority—unless constituted authority
set itself against me. Then I, naturally, would
demand my rights. (My rights, at the last in-
ventory, consisted of the right to inhale and
exhale, and to wear the top button of my coat
buttoned.)

But I do protest against the Cossack rule of
the statisticians. Supposing that, right now, I
should decide that I wanted to be the father of
sextuplets, and had a pretty good idea of how
to set about it. Would the fact that sextuplets

had already been born in Inotest, Rumania, hold me back, just because there had not been five billion single babies born since that date? No, *citoyens*, I am a free agent! I happen not to *want* to be the father of sextuplets, which is the only reason that I am not an outlaw.

* * * * *

And there is a point which the promulgators of the oppressive "Rule of 87" have possibly never considered. Only one father—or mother— in five billion *wants* to promote sextuplets. Think that over on your legislator!

Jolly Good
Fellows

AT A dinner of the Dante Society in London several years ago the Poet Laureate of England had proposed the toast and the toast-master had given his all to the announcement: "Ladies and gentlemen—the toast is Dante!"

There was a slight pause, and then the pianist, feeling that something was expected of him, crashed through with "For He's a Jolly Good Fellow!"

The same thing happened only recently to the Bishop of London. "On rising to reply," says a newspaper account, "he was received with loud cheers and the singing of 'For He's a Jolly Good Fellow.'"

*   *   *   *   *

The same thing happens in the United States every time a group of men (and, Heaven help us, sometimes women, too) feel like paying especial tribute to some poor guy who wishes he were dead at that very moment.

224

In the first place, no words could be less appropriate, and everybody feels this fact as he finds himself singing them. That is why everybody is so embarrassed and so glad when the whole horrid affair is over. Even the incorrigible song-leader who has struck it up must wish, by the time he has reached the third "For He's a Jolly Good Fellow" that he had not got quite so hearty.

I don't know in which case the words, "jolly good fellow" are more embarrassing, in the case of Dante and the Bishop of London or in the case of some tough mug who is being feted for having won the heavyweight championship of the Navy. I think that probably the latter blushes more. Anyone calling him a "jolly good fellow" to his face would have to take the consequences.

* * * * *

For a nation of people who are so crazy mad about giving each other testimonial dinners we have a remarkable paucity of virile, up-to-date song tributes. They all seem to have been composed in 1870, when people made puns in Latin and Greek, and it was considered pretty devilish to lead a cow up in the chapel bell tower. Even

*Even the song-leader must wish
he had not got quite so hearty*

the music dates back to Sir Arthur Sullivan and
the days when Marlborough was taking himself
off to war.

Take, as another example, the drinking song
beginning: "Here's to Blevitch, he's true blue!"
True blue! What kind of talk is that for a
bunch of 1936 drunks?

And the last line: "When he wants to get to
heaven, he will go the other way!" Do you suppose that they mean "H—l?"

"Hail, Hail, the Gang's All Here!" does manage to keep in the vernacular pretty well for an
old number, but, even in that, all but the most
emancipated singers say "What the heck do we
care?" And "Hail, hail!" is not a paean of praise

226

to any one person, anyway. It is every man for himself as the hero.

*　*　*　*　*

The point is that we have outgrown the old formal group toast-to-music and don't know it. That is why nobody writes any new ones. That is why it is so embarrassing to sing the old ones.

If we have to sing at testimonial dinners let it be "Down by the Old Mill Stream," with no names mentioned.

Taking Up the Cudgels

SOMEBODY named Sir Shah Sulaiman, of Allahabad, India, has seen fit to challenge Professor Albert Einstein's Theory of Relativity. In the absence of Professor Einstein, I am taking the liberty of replying in his behalf.

Einstein's value of the deflection of light from a star as it comes past the sun is 1.75. Sir Shah Sulaiman's prediction of value is between 2.32 and 2.45.

My answer to Sir S. S.: You're crazy.

Einstein's value of the amount of shifting towards red of the spectrum of the light from the limb of the sun is: .0084. Sir S. S. predicts that it will be found to be .00676.

My answer: Poppycock.

Sir S. S.'s third prediction concerns the elements of orbits of planets. He says that the value for the advance of the perihelion of planet Mercury is less than estimated by Newcomb.

My answer: Where is Allahabad, India, anyway? And who asked *you* to butt in on this? We were getting along very nicely with Prof.

228

Einstein, who has proven himself to be an extremely pleasant gentleman and an all-around good egg. He also plays the violin. What can *you* play?

* * * * *

That is the trouble with discovering something worth while. Sooner or later some fly-by-night chief justice of India (that's what Sir Shah is, a chief justice) comes along and says that you are all wrong, and that he has discovered something better that will also cure head colds. It's enough to make a man like Einstein throw the whole thing up and just sail boats all the rest of his life.

Of course, it's none of my business, but, being in more or less the same line of work as Einstein (writing), I feel that we all ought to stand together.

Prof. Einstein probably will have something more to add to his own defense than what I have outlined here, but this will serve as an opening gun in the rebuttal.

I also hereby offer to meet Sir Shah in public debate.

Special Sale!

IN THE welter of disturbing dispatches from overseas, the following item from the London *Observer* is vaguely reassuring:

"A recent paragraph (here) mentioned the sale by Robert Hope-Johnson of his moustache to Lord Esme Gordon at the old Pelican Club, and speculated as to the fate of the ornament."

This, in a way, calms everything down. Not only the fact that Robert Hope-Johnson could sell his moustache to Lord Esme Gordon at the Pelican Club, but the fact that the *Observer* could speculate "as to the fate of the ornament" in times like these, lends a sort of common sense to the affairs of the world which they sadly need.

Furthermore, the *Observer* is happy to state that it has been informed by a correspondent that "the hirsute relics were sent to Rowland Ward, who mounted them in a case of velvet and silver, with a suitable lyric inscription appended, and the trophy occupied a place of honor upon the walls of the club."

The correspondent adds that the famous moustache of Mr. Herman-Hodge (now Lord Wyfold) "is, I am pleased to say, as fine as ever."

* * * * *

There is, obviously, more here than meets the eye of the American reader. This barter of rare moustaches is evidently something that causes no more comment among British club-men than the exchange of a stuffed boar's head for three dick-dick antlers. The spirit behind the whole thing seems charming.

But what is confusing is, if Mr. Hope-Johnson possessed such a spectacular set of moustaches, why did he feel that he must sell them to Lord Esme Gordon? Was it in payment of some old gambling debt, or had they belonged to Lord Esme in the first place and were only farmed out?

And why sell them instead of paying rent? And what is Mr. Hope-Johnson doing now? Surely he can raise another set and sell them for more.

What I want to see is a photograph of Mr. Hope-Johnson before he went commercial.

All Aboard
for Dementia Praecox

IT IS a little terrifying, with all that I have to do this week, to discover that I have a *dementia praecox* into the bargain. "What next?" I often ask myself.

There is no doubt about the *dementia praecox*. I've got it, all right. The only question now is, can I swing the other things that I have to face? A good case of *dementia praecox* is about enough for one week.

I got my data from a report submitted at the American Psychiatric Association. This report said that *dementia praecox* can be helped by oxygen treatment. And, in passing, the report just happened to mention the symptoms of *dementia praecox*. Not that any of its readers would find it applicable to themselves—just in passing, you know.

Early stages: (1) "Defective judgment." Well, I could keep you here all night giving examples of my defective judgment that would make your blood curdle. I couldn't even judge a sack-race. On this count I qualify hands down.

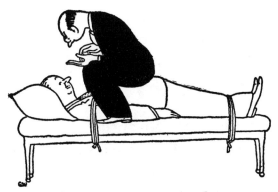

Even then my eyes wander

(2) "Retarded perception." I didn't even know that the fleet was in until I read *Time* ten days later.

(3) "Restrictions in the field of attention." My attention can be held only by strapping me down to a cot and sitting on my chest. Even then my eyes wander.

(4) "Deficiency of ethical inhibitions." I took a course in ethics once, but I didn't do very well in it. We didn't know about "inhibitions" in my day. They came in with horn-rimmed glasses and Freud. We just said "Yes, please," or "No, thanks," and let it go at that. I don't know whether I've got "ethical inhibitions" or not. Just try me once, that's all.

(5) "Silly laughter." I hold the Interscholastic (New England), Intercollegiate, East Coast

Amateur and Open Professional cups for silly laughter. I laugh at anything except a French clown. You can't be sillier than that.

*   *   *   *   *

Among the more advanced symptoms of *dementia praecox* I find to my horror the following:

(1) "Lack of skill in motor performance." I was asked to surrender my license while driving an old Model T Ford in 1915 because I could not co-ordinate in time to press the clutch at just the right moment. I also had a little trouble with "right" and "left." Next to "silly laughter," "lack of skill in motor performance" is my forte.

(2) "Stupor." We need not go into this. The last thing that I remember clearly is that elaborate parade for Admiral Dewey under the arch at Twenty-third street. Since then I have more or less taken things easily. In addition, I can say only that there are hundreds of people willing to bet that I have *never* had my eyes open. I have no proof to the contrary.

So *dementia praecox* it is, boys! And may the best man win!

For Release Monday

OUR Publicity Department submits the following items of interest (of interest to our Publicity Department) concerning a few of our authors. In case you do not want to print them, they go awfully well with peanut butter.

* * * * *

How does an author work when he has been put in a strait-jacket by relatives? This question is answered by Germer C. Arsh, author of "Brimmer Grows a Goatee and Other Sonnets," to be published in the Fall by the Aesophagus Press. "I just lie there and think very hard," he says, "and pretty soon the book is written by my sister."

* * * * *

Lingard M. Lilacs, author of "Penny Wise, Pound of Cat Meat," to be published in the Fall by the Aesophagus Press, is probably the only short, blond man to be taken for Primo Carnera. He was taken for Carnera, along with a dozen Easter eggs, but Carnera couldn't see his way clear to using any of them.

*   *   *   *   *

"Never try to set a thief to catch a thief, or to throw good money after bad," says Robert Wrist, in the third chapter of "Don't Open on Christmas!" (Aesophagus Press.) "I am sick and tired of trying." Mr. Wrist's book is now in its first edition.

*   *   *   *   *

Quite a controversy has arisen, and died down, over Marian Querey's statement that women are more allergic to horsehairs than men. "I can't go near a horse," said Miss Querey, "without sneezing, due to the fine particles of horsehair that are in the air. I know lots of girls who are the same way but only one man." The answer is, according to our opponents, that Miss Querey knows only one man anyway.

Miss Querey's new book, *April Asthma*, will be published in the Fall by the Aesophagus Press.

*   *   *   *   *

"Arabian is the easiest language in the world

to Iearn, next to Choctaw," says the Princess Ludovica von Preepos und Schnurbart, whose novel, *Tight Grows the Eel-Grass,* is already being considered for rejection by the Aesophagus Press. "All you have to do is remember that all verbs meaning 'to inhale' take the dative."

*　*　*　*　*

Remember, all of these items are absolutely free for your use, together with libel liability and a big kiss.

One Minute, Please

ABOUT an hour ago the telephone bell rang. I answered it after a fashion.

A very brisk young woman said, "Wait a minute, please," but she didn't mean the "please." What she obviously meant was just "Wait a minute!"

Now this is a thing that especially irks me. When I am called by a secretary who doesn't tell me who is calling, but says, "Wait a minute" and then goes off somewhere for five minutes, I hang up.

So I hung up. "They'll call back," I said to myself, and stood waiting by the instrument.

I tried to read the paper I had in my hand, but couldn't concentrate. Each second I could hear that bell ringing, only it didn't ring. I sat down by the telephone. "There's no sense in going back into the other room," I thought. "It'll come any minute now." But it didn't.

* * * * *

The sound of a telephone bell which ought

I couldn't concentrate

to ring any minute, but doesn't, is much worse than the actual thing. By this time I was definitely on edge. I was also in a frenzy to know who the caller had been.

Finally I went into the other room. "That'll bring them," I said to myself, sagely. I know how those things work.

But I overestimated their perversity this time. Even when I sat down in a low, easy chair, difficult to get out of, it didn't work. As a final ruse I lay down on a couch and pretended to be asleep. No bell.

I thought of calling Central and asking who

had called me, but that would be weak. Anyway, Central couldn't tell me. I thought of calling all my friends and asking them if they had
just called, but that would be pretty futile on
the face of it. I thought of putting the whole
matter out of my mind, but that was impossible. I was obsessed.

*　　*　　*　　*　　*

It has been an hour now and I have been
pacing up and down the room gnawing at my
nails. Obviously whoever it was is *not* going to
call back. In a weak attempt to restore my peace
of mind I am using this space as a

PERSONAL COLUMN

At five-thirty on the afternoon of Tuesday,
June 25, *who called me on the telephone?*

Who Did It?

THE parlor game of "Detective" got off to a flying start a few months ago, but what it needs now are some fresh problems. Not having any personal problems of my own I am taking the liberty of making up a few:

1. A man leaves his home in the morning to go to work. An hour later he is found back in his own bed with a nasty scalp wound. His clothes are folded neatly over a chair. He is unable to talk, but a colored man, who is in bed with him, also with a bad scalp wound, says that he doesn't know who his buddie is, having never seen him before. The police arrest the housekeeper. Why?

Answer: Because she was a notorious counterfeiter.

* * * * *

2. A baggage master in a small railway station detects something suspicious about a large box which has been lying in the baggage room for three years. He opens it and finds a mummi-

fied fox terrier. Around the dog's neck is a tag reading: "Please return to John Grunch, 78 North Creep Street, Noky, Idaho."

The police go to the address and are told that Mr. Grunch doesn't live there any more. What should the next move be?

Answer: Try 356 Welkin Drive and ring Dunker's bell.

* * * * *

3. Three men are sitting at a table playing "gummidge." A says: "I have seven stops." B says: "I have three leaves and a throw." C says: "I win! I have two reekers." There is only one reeker in a "gummidge" pack. Who won?

Answer: Joe Louis.

Prodigal
Sea-Lions

TWO letters written to the bedeviled editor
of the *London Sunday Times* have stirred
old memories in my breast, and if the editor
of the *Sunday Times* doesn't mind I will take
them off his hands.

The first, from a Mr. Ernest Blaikley, of Stan-
ley Gardens, N. W. 3, begins: "Recently, at a
well-known circus, I saw the performing sea-
lions. As I watched their extraordinary balancing feats I could not help wondering to what
use they put this peculiar gift in their wild
state."

Without knowing it, Mr. Blaikley has hit
upon a very tender subject with me. It has to
do with my first job after leaving college, and
therefore my first failure at a job. On "coming
down" from the university I was employed by
an oil spermery-and-refining company, to do
just exactly what Mr. Blaikley has been wondering about. I was assigned the job of finding out
some use for the peculiar balancing gift of sea-
lions.

*   *   *   *   *

243

Of course, my company was concerned primarily with whales and their by-products, but it had been found that the seals in the whaling territory were seriously impeding operations by sitting around in the way of the whalers and just swinging back and forth with their noses in the air. "Find those animals something to balance on their noses," said the captain of the whaling fleet in his monthly report, "or I shall go crazy."

So I went up into the seal district and tried putting various light objects on the noses of the seals as they swung back and forth. This is very hard to do, you will find. I tried the conventional rubber ball, but discovered that it is only seals with actor-blood in their veins that will go for the rubber ball. The ones we see in circuses are dyed-in-the-wool hams, who like to show off and revel in public applause. Your average sea-lion, the sea-lion-in-the-street, doesn't give a hoot whether anyone sees him or not—and I shouldn't think that he would, everything considered.

So you will see that my assignment was not an easy one, for not only was I unable to get the seals to hold still enough for me to get anything started balancing on their noses, but I couldn't make them see the importance of trying to balance things for themselves. They just didn't seem to care that they had this peculiar gift (which Mr. Blaikley has noticed, too, and wondered about), or that it was going to waste. And you just can't help anyone who refuses to help himself. Any social worker will tell you that.

So I simply sent in my report, which read: "Complete indifference on part of seals to waste of balancing gift. Recommend abandoning whole project." Naturally, I was not given another assignment, and if Mr. Blaikley wants to take a try at it my old desk is still vacant, I understand.

*　　*　　*　　*　　*

The other letter to the *Sunday Times* deals with a controversy which has been raging over the site, and name, of the earliest indoor skating rink in London, and I am afraid that I have not left quite room enough to take it up now. Perhaps at our next session we can deal with it. In the meantime I will go over my records more carefully, for I am a little hazy on one or two points. We might all of us read up a bit on Early Indoor Skating Rinks of London, and then I shall not be talking to such a lot of lunkheads on the subject as might otherwise be the case.

London's
Oldest Rink

I F YOU don't mind, we will now take up the second of two letters to the *London Sunday Times* which held me spellbound when I first read them, the other having been apropos the lack of things for seals to balance on their noses when in their wild state.

The letter which we will use as a basis for today's seminar is from Sir Algernon Law, and reads as follows:

"Sir—it must have been in the mid-seventies that Mr. Gamgee started his indoor ice-rink off the King's Road, Chelsea. My brothers, Major (later Major-General) F. T. A. Law and Mr. Ernest Law, used to skate there. But it was poorly attended. When my brother Ernest came in the afternoon, he would ask: 'Has anyone been here?' The reply would often be: 'Only the marquess and the major!'

"The marquess was Clanricarde, a timid performer, who used to fly from the brusque movements of the major, who had learnt to skate on the Peiho River in 1861. As the 'major' became a lieut.-colonel on October 1, 1877, Mr. Gamgee's venture was apparently the earliest of its kind in this country."

*　*　*　*　*

Sir Algernon is cockeyed. The first indoor skating rink in London was not Mr. Gamgee's comparatively modern venture, but one situated in the old Baker Street Bazaar, adjoining the original Madame Tussaud's Exhibition. This flourished in 1845, when Sir Algernon's Mr. Gamgee (granting that there could have been a person named Gamgee) was a mere child, and probably a very disagreeable child, too.

My grandfather, Corporal Benchley (later Private Benchley) used to skate there and has left abundant correspondence to prove it. Almost anything can be proved by my grandfather's correspondence, as he liked to write, and was interested in practically everything. A lot of it he wrote in a jaunting-car, however, which makes it read almost like music.

*　*　*　*　*

However, I have before me a note made by him in 1845, just previous to his falling down in the old Baker Street Rink. It reads: "I guess I'll fall down now—Boomp! There I go!"

In his diary, under a date which seems to be 1456, but couldn't be, he writes: "When I went to the rink to skate today, I asked the Duke of Chichester, who sweeps off the ice, if anyone had fallen down more often than I had the day before. 'Dey's nobody here but jes' us chickens!' replied the old Duke, referring to a Negro story current at the time. So we joined hands and skated around the rink once together, then backwards as far as we were able, which, I am convulsed to say, wasn't very far."

This makes it clear, I think, that indoor ice-skating was already an established fad in London as early as 1845, or, if we take the date in my grandfather's diary as authentic, 1456. In 1456, however, the Wars of the Roses were just beginning and it wouldn't have been cold enough for much skating. And I am sure that my grandfather was not four hundred and four years old when he died in 1860, or we kids would have been told something about it.

I think that I have shown enough to prove Sir Algernon Law wrong, with his Mr. Gamgee and 1877, and, unless the British aristocracy has gone completely to pot, he will apologize.

Robot
Rats

IT'S all right with me if people want to con-struct robots to do the work of men. In fact, I could use a good robot right this minute. But I can't see the sense of making robot rats.

Some one has gone and made a robot rat. Maybe it is because I don't quite understand what they are going to use a robot rat for, but the whole thing seems to be a little unneces-sary. I don't like rats anyway.

This "rat" is described as a sort of "three-wheeled roller skate, loaded with small motors, electromagnets and switches," which, I will ad-mit, must be an improvement over the ordi-nary house, or wharf, rat in appearance. It shouldn't send timid folks leaping into chairs at any rate.

But I still can't figure out the need for hav-ing done it at all. The robot rat is so con-structed that, when set on a track and adjusted to take the wrong turn at a switch, it learns a lesson from having bumped up the dead-end

249

and the next time takes the right turn of its own accord.

This is very cute of it, but wouldn't it have been simpler to have adjusted it to take the right turn in the *first* place? Why subject it to the humiliation of bumping up the dead-end at all?

* * * * *

I don't know anything at all about machinery, and I am sure that the whole thing has a purpose and a very valuable one. (The end of the article I read about it was torn off, so I just got the main idea without the explanation of why it was considered necessary.)

I do know that, for the present, there are several mechanical appliances that I want more than a robot rat which is deliberately maladjusted just for the sake of watching it do the whole thing over again correctly. If anyone does give me one for Christmas I warn the scientific world that I will fix it to take the *correct* turn the first time, thereby spoiling the experiment.

I will also change the name from "rat" to "roller skate."

End of
the Chanticleer!

FOR the benefit of those who find themselves unable to sleep through the early-
morning clarion call of the rooster (sometimes
called "The Herald of the Dawn," among other
names), I will recount how I, single-handed,
put an end to this chanticleer business for at
least one morning.

In telling my story I may have to make myself seem to be cutting a rather strange figure,
but I am willing to be misunderstood if I can
spread the word that the Lord of the Barnyard
need no longer also be the Lord of the Bedroom, and that a man, by striking out with
some spirit, can meet a rooster in single com-
bat, and win.

* * * * *

Returning home late from a Grange meeting, I was shown to the guest-room which, as it
turned out, was abutting the poultry reserva-
tion. I had barely found my pillow (it was a
small one and easily lost) and closed my eyes

251

(also small and easily lost) when Sir Rooster began to put on his act. "Cock-a-doodle-do" is the way it is printed, but that is a euphemism.

At first I thought that the bird was in bed with me, but, after a careful pawing with my hands and feet, I decided that he was outside. It then became a matter for direct action on my part. With a determination which I seldom display in crises, I got out of bed and, putting on the tops of my pajamas, went out into the hen-yard.

I took my stand by the wire enclosure and waited. Several of the hens paid me the courtesy of a glance, but the rooster was gathering himself for another onslaught at the silences and did not see me. I was calmness itself.

*   *   *   *   *

Then it came—a rousing, throaty crow, which he doubtless thought was causing me to writhe on my couch inside the guest-house. I did not leave him long in his fool's paradise. I answered him with a louder and throatier crow which practically tore my tonsils from their moorings, but which also sent my antagonist toppling to one side in surprise and chagrin. The battle was on!

Every time he crowed I would crow back,

going him one better. Once I even carried the fight into his own territory and crowed first. This sent him into a fever of inferiority, believe it or not. The Cock of the Walk befuddled, confused, and a tantrum of futility!

The hens took it rather hard. Not only were they being terrified personally (I saw to that, in my odd moments), but their hero was being mocked, ridiculed, and outplayed at his own game. They ran to and fro in despair, but I was not to be put off by any considerations of chivalry. I even did a few hen cackles to put *them* in *their* places. It was a complete rout in favor of the forces of law and order.

* * * * *

It was not long before I waited in vain for a "cock-a-doodle-do" to set me off into my own. The rooster was licked and he knew it. A few hens were still loyal to him and tried to curry favor by running back to him and saying, "The man's drunk! Pay no attention to him." But I wasn't drunk, unless it was with power, and the Old Devil knew it.

So, still in the tops of my pajamas, I made my triumphal entry back into the guest-house and took a well-deserved nap, with no sound from the hen-yard except a few scattered cluckings from discontented poultry who were talking it over. The Big Shot was silent, probably committing suicide.

I found out at luncheon, however, that I had awakened everyone else in the household, which somehow was never completely under the spell of the illusion that I was a rooster. Well, in every great cause some few innocent heads must fall.

Waiting
for Bad News

E VER since last Summer I have been waiting for a decision in a case which affects
me rather seriously. Is there, or is there not,
such a thing as a tribal pow-wow of prairie
chickens? If there is, I'm through!

I read of it first in *Time*, although it is evidently an age-old custom—or a superstition.
That's what I want to know—is it a custom or
a superstition? *Time* said that it was a superstition, and then someone wrote in and said that
it was on the level. I haven't slept a wink since.

*   *   *   *   *

For the benefit of those who do not know
what a prairie chicken pow-wow is I will quote
from *Time's* disturbing account of what three
men saw on a prairie in Saskatchewan, one of
the men being an ex-premier of that province.

"In double file, with every one in step, twenty
black-and-white streaked grouse strutted forward, keeping perfect time. As one they hopped
as neatly back. Forward again, and with heads

255

bobbing the two front couples swung to left and right, wheeled fanwise, fell in at the rear. Four times the figure was repeated, until the rear couples were once more in their places. Now odd couples did a left face, even couples a right face, and the two lines moved apart. An about-face brought them back together. Then all faced front and again the double file moved forward—one, two, three, four; one, two, three, four."

Superstition or not, it isn't reassuring to know that anyone could even *think* he saw that! I don't like even to copy it out.

* * * * *

But then somebody wrote into *Time* and said that it wasn't a superstition at all, and gave some sort of explanation for it, having to do, I think, with mating time. I remember reading it hurriedly and thinking: "I'll study this later, when I'm feeling better." And then I lost it.

That was during the Summer, and here it is almost Winter and I am still in the dark about it. Do prairie chickens do a Portland Fancy in groups of twenty or don't they? It sometimes seems as if I should go mad worrying about it!

Time said it was a myth, handed down from the Indians, and that people in Saskatchewan

I pray I don't end up in the middle of my bedroom floor doing the steps myself

didn't believe it any more. Then this man wrote in and said that it was a well-known fact. And the ex-premier and two other men swore that they saw it from their automobile. Nothing further has come out about it. That's where the matter stands—it may, or it may not, be true. It's the uncertainty of the thing!

    ＊   ＊   ＊   ＊   ＊

I put out my light each night and try to think of church picnics when I was a child and of the quiet streets of Rothenburg, Germany. I run over the score of *Iolanthe* and try to remember the members of my class in the Fourth Grade. I say to myself: "You are your own worst enemy if you let yourself think of prairie chickens!"

But in spite of all this the prairie chickens come, all twenty of them, in double file, with every one in step. Forward and back, first couples to the right, second to the left, "ladies change" (or was it "ladies' chain"?) and "balance your partners!" Then, "All face Benchley! March! One, two, three, four; one, two, three, four!" It is horrible!

It's the backward steps that terrify me the most. Birds shouldn't take steps forward and *then* steps backward—*in tempo!* They shouldn't take steps backward anyway, not even in a myth.

*   *   *   *   *

I am writing this in the hope that the man who wrote to *Time* will see it and put me out of my misery. If such a thing exists I might as well know it and make my plans accordingly.

All that I pray is, when the truth is broken to me, I don't end up in the middle of my bedroom floor doing the steps myself.

Judgment-Day
Rehearsal

FATE, that saucy minx, has ordained that, for the past three Summers, I should live in a section of the country where thunderstorms are practically unknown. *(Note to Chamber of Commerce: How about a parking permit, boys?)*

This has been all right with me, as I list thunderstorms eighteenth in my category of favorite pranks of Nature. There is something tricky about a thunderstorm that I don't like. Three Summers without one have been so much velvet.

Yesterday morning, however, I was awakened by the sound of thunder. A morning thunderstorm, in any section of the country, is an ominous piece of business. When you haven't heard thunder for three years it has somewhat the effect on the pores as the sound of Gabriel's trumpet.

At first I thought that it was an earthquake. *(Note to Chamber of Commerce: Never mind about that parking permit.)* I had heard that

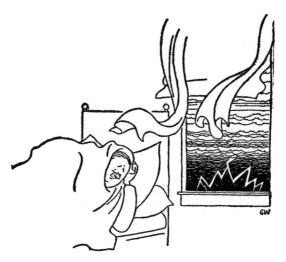

*There is something tricky about a thunderstorm
that I don't like*

earthquakes sound like thunder at first, so I watched the pictures on the wall like a hawk. Not a very alert hawk, I will admit, for I dozed off almost immediately.

Then the rumble came again, this time nearer, and I decided that it wasn't an earthquake. I was rather disappointed, in a way, as I sleep on the ground floor and am fairly agile, in spite of my enormous weight. Agility counts for nothing in a thunderstorm.

* * * * *

As the storm came nearer I began to realize

that I hadn't made the most of my three years' immunity. In fact, I hadn't done a single thing about cleaning up my life. I was, if anything, an even more logical target for lightning than the last time I was within range. And thunderstorms don't creep up on you at seven o'clock in the morning in a non-thunderstorm country for nothing, you know.

I lined up a rather panicky schedule of reforms which I would put into effect if I got out of this scrape without being made the focal point for an electrical display. It involved what is known in municipal circles as a "clean-up in all departments."

But as the storm suddenly petered out and went off in the other direction nothing much has come out of it yet. I may have three years more, and these things can't be rushed.

What
to Loll In

THE problem of what to wear while lolling about the house on a hot Sunday afternoon is becoming more and more acute as the fashions in lolling garments change. The American home is in danger of taking on the appearance of an Oriental bordello.

There was a time when on a hot Sunday afternoon the various members of the family retired to their respective rooms and just plain "stripped down." It wasn't a family group that John Singer Sargent would have wasted much time over, but it kept the air currents passing back and forth over the epidermis.

There were several drawbacks to this nudist policy, however. It more or less prevented games of bridge and group singing, and caused the house to ring with cries of, "Keep out of here, will you!"

It also made it difficult to find places to sit down. Chairs and sofas developed unsuspected bristles, and one had more or less to keep walking up and down while reading, unless there happened to be an old-fashioned, cool-surfaced horsehair sofa handy. Even then there were several spots on its surface that had to be watched.

But with the advent of fancy beach togs and diaphanous sports rigs it became possible to wear something that passed for clothing and yet to keep cool. Unfortunately, however, these exotic-looking outfits were designed for use on beaches, where yellow sands and blue waves and multi-colored umbrellas make them a bit less conspicuous. They do *not* go well in a city apartment, or a country cottage, on a Sunday afternoon.

* * * * *

On such Sundays as the family are not at the beach or at the swimming-pool, the living-room becomes the scene of what might be a Pagan rout, if there were any rout. We see Mother and the girls arrayed as if they were about to be sold at auction, prosaically reading the Sunday papers, while Daddy and the boys moon about, like the Pirates of Penzance, in gay stripes and flaming bandanas, cool, perhaps, but obviously on the lookout for a dance boat on a Venetian lagoon.

It is the effect on the family morale that is the danger of this home masquerade. Everyone is at home, but is dressed for somewhere else. The furniture seems shabby. The four walls close in. Personalities clash and fist fights set in.

It would be much better if everyone went to his room and stripped, as Grandpa used to do.

Blizzard
Hysteria

FROM my seat in a snow-bank, where I happened to be taking it easy last week for a minute before starting to look for my right shoe again, I laughingly remembered a threat that I made early in October.

"If we don't get any more snow this Winter than we have had the past five years, I am packing up and going to Canada for a month. I'm a snow-baby," I said, ruggedly, "and I'm going to get some snow for myself this year or know the reason why."

Well, I got my snow, and without having to go any nearer Canada than the north windows of my house. Sometimes I couldn't even get within two feet of my north windows.

* * * * *

I shall be particularly glad this year when it stops blizzarding, as then we won't have so much trouble with Joe. Joe is a friend of mine who gets blizzard hysteria. As soon as a real blizzard sets in, he goes St. Bernard on us.

265

The only difference between him and the famous mountain dogs is that, instead of the St. Bernard going out to look for lost travelers in the snow, we all have to go out in the snow and look for the St. Bernard. The only feature of the old St. Bernard tradition that he has retained is the keg of brandy around his neck.

*　　*　　*　　*　　*

When the first blizzard of the present season started, I noticed a strange light come into Joe's eye. He went to the window and looked out at the whirling snow, and I saw his left foot start to paw around slightly. "Looks like a real one," he said. Then, after a pause, he repeated: "Yes, sir! A real one!" This was around lunch time.

"I guess I'll get out the team," he said, softly, "and mush up to Jack and Charlie's for a bite to eat." That was the last I saw of him until Thursday.

Later that afternoon, I did get a report from him. He called on the telephone and said, in a voice quivering with excitement: "Come on out and play, you old stick-in-the-mud, you! The snow's a foot deep!" I asked him where he was, and he said "Latitude 45—Longitude 54."

In about an hour he called up again and said that the horses were all down in the streets and that Shearer's Dry Goods Store was on fire. "Get your sled and come on out!" was his final shout, as he hung up. In a field-communique along about six, he announced that shipping was tied up and that he didn't think he could bring the "Sarah H. Walton" in until morning. At ten that night his wife called up and asked if I knew where Joe was.

* * * * *

On Thursday, Joe was very dispirited. "I don't see how it could have happened," he said. "I don't know anybody in New Rochelle." We both agreed that a little vacation once every ten years or so did a man no harm, especially, as Joe said, as it would be ten years before we had another blizzard. As he said this he walked to the window, and I heard him moan. It was snowing again.

"I guess I'd better get home before it gets too deep," said Joe. This was about four in the afternoon. At six he called up and said: "Get your sled out! This looks like a real one!"

This time we got the searching parties out early, but it was hard going and he got to Montclair, New Jersey, before we caught him. He had built himself a snow fort and kept us at bay with snow-balls for quite a while.

And so it has gone all Winter. Much as I like snow, I dread to see each successive blizzard starting, for it means a night out with the dog sleds. Joe himself dreads it more than we do, and hides under the bed whenever he sees the first flakes come swirling down. But he can't seem to win out. This year, Spring will have a doubly grateful significance for everyone, I guess.

The Moth Invasion

O NE day, a few weeks ago, certain sections of New York City found themselves in the midst of a flurry of tiny, white moths. A lot of people thought at first that it was snow, but as the thermometer read 97 at the moment, this theory was discarded as visionary.

It has been my great good luck to talk with one of the moths himself, one who got separated from the swarm and flew in at my window. Being rather unnerved by his experience, he felt that he wanted to talk to somebody about it. He gave me quite a different angle on the Big Moth Invasion of 1935.

"We were flying along, the rest of the bunch and I," he said, "when, all of a sudden, the air ahead of us seemed full of great, hulking shapes impeding our passage.

"Harry, my pal, who was flying alongside of me, took one look and said: 'Hello, what's all this? A phenomenon?'

"I could hardly see a wing before my face for the great swarm of woolen-covered bodies that pushed up against us, and, for a moment, I thought that Harry was right. 'A phenomenon as ever I saw,' I said. 'Just pay no attention, Harry, and we'll be out of it in a minute.'

*　　*　　*　　*　　*

"Then one of the boys, who had studied anthropology in school, spoke up and said that it was nothing but a settlement of human beings, who, on hot days, sometimes appear in large numbers and beat themselves blindly against whatever happens to be in their way. 'We just happen to have run into a bit of hard luck,' he added.

"Well, sir, we flew along for a while, and these things seemed to get thicker and thicker. One of them, lunging ahead right in front of me, caught me plumb in the eye, so that I couldn't see for a minute.

" 'Let's fly out of here!' I yelled to Harry and the rest of the boys. 'I can't take it. Let's get a little altitude and see if we can't fly over it!'

"But Harry had caught one of those New Yorkers (the special breed of human that was proving such a pain in the neck to us) right by the windshield of his automobile, and couldn't get him loose. 'This guy is blinding

me!' he yelled back at me. Things were beginning to look pretty serious.

*   *   *   *   *

"So I ups and turns into a sharp left at about
fifty feet, and, the next thing I know I'm
through the window and here in your office.
. . . Got a drink?"

I gave him a hooker of straight rye.

"That's better," he said, coughing. "Do you
have these things around here much?"

"Quite a bit," I said. "They come out with
the sunshine."

"O. K.," said the moth, poising himself on
the window ledge. "Next time I'll make a de-
tour. What's the name of this place again?"

"New York," I replied.

"That's right. New York! I ought to remember that—my mother was a Yorkshire Gypsy.
Well, toodle-oo! I'll be seein' yer!" And he was
off to join his squadron.

Don't
Get Lost!

I F YOU are one of those helpless people who
are constantly getting lost, and just standing
still and sobbing, the coming season holds out
great hope for you. The stars are going to be
unusually bright this Summer. You can't get
lost if you know the stars—unless, of course, you
can't see the stars.

People usually get lost more easily in Summer than they do in Winter, because they find
themselves in stranger places in Summer. Anyone who, in Winter, gets lost in his own street,
or even five blocks from his own street (which
is as far away as any sensible man gets in Winter), will not be benefited by looking at any
stars. What he needs is a nice, sympathetic
cop.

But in the Summer you get to stumbling
around in fields, or on the beach looking for
horseshoe-crabs, and, along about eleven o'clock
in the evening, you are quite likely to find yourself tripping over an old cigaret-butt of yours
that you dropped half an hour before on the

*Say to yourself, "Jupi-
ter should be right over
our house"*

way home. Anyone is likely to do that, so don't
get downhearted. You're nobody's fool.

*   *   *   *   *

If you find yourself lost during the last two
weeks of July (you have simply got to know, in
a general way, what time of the month it is, or

273

I can be of no help to you), look in the skies for the brightest star, which will be Jupiter. Then you can say: "That's Jupiter!" So far, so good.

Now, work backward. I don't mean *walk* backward, but say to yourself: "Jupiter should be right over our house—a little to the left." You will have to have figured this out before leaving the house, but that's the fun of the thing. There will be so much figuring out to do before you leave the house that you may not leave at all, and then you won't even get lost.

Therefore, if Jupiter is right over your house and a little to the left, the thing for you to do now is to walk, very carefully, toward Jupiter— and a little to the right. This will land you nicely in the old north creek.

*   *   *   *   *

Or, if you happen to get lost during the middle of August (between the 11th and the 21st, to be exact—don't count on it if it happens to be the 22nd), you must look for Venus. Venus is unusually bright just after sunset, so lay your plans to get lost just after sunset. All you have to know is just what relation Venus bears to the spot you are headed for and—presto—there you are—still lost!

*Of course if you get lost indoors
it will do you no good*

Of course, if you get lost indoors, in a strange house, and can't find the bathroom, it will do you no good to stick your head out the window to look for a star. Neither can you count on the heavens if you find yourself lost in your own bed, with the footboard where the headboard ought to be. In such emergencies as these you will simply have to use your wits.

But, in general, there is no excuse for a good woodsman or a good mariner getting lost in the Summer time, unless, of course, he *wants* to get lost. That can happen, too.

275

Notes

HENRI LABABAGE, the inventor of crêpes Suzette, arrived in town today, parcel post. His version of the invention of the famous dessert is a simple and wholly credible one:

"I was chef at the Sulphur Baths at Oxnard," he said, blushing furiously. "King Edward VII, then known to his intimates as the Prince de Galles, came to me and he say: 'Henri,' he say, 'make me a crêpe Suzette!' So I make him three crêpes Suzette. *Voici!*"

*   *   *   *   *

Campari Janos, famous Hungarian maître d'hôtel, was talking the other night in front of a mirror. There were a lot of us sitting around, singing gypsy songs ("Hi-ya!") and going to town.

"Who is that mysterious-looking ingot?" asked someone, doubtless I (or me) pointing to Janos.

"That is the inventor of crêpes Suzette," was the reply, scarcely audible over the reflexes. "He named them after Suzette, a famous *pot au feu* of his day."

* * * * *

"You ask me how I came to invent crêpes Suzette," said Hyman Shrink, opening his vest. "I am telling you.

"I was a stranger in town and so was the Prince of Wales, then known as King Edward VII to his intimates. He asked me why I didn't make a pancake which would taste like an orange, only with a pancake flavor.

"'Why don't *you?*' I asked him right back.

"But finally he wheedled me into doing it, and that is how crêpe Suzettes were invented."

* * * * *

A man who was arrested at the corner of Sixth ave., New York, and Michigan blvd., Chicago, yesterday, on the charge of being too alert-looking, told the jail matron that he was the inventor of crêpes Suzette.

"I was King Edward at the time," he replied, "and it seemed to be the only thing to do. Suzette was one swell gal."

* * * * *

As a matter of fact, *I* invented crêpes Suzette, and I did it by getting so gosh-darned sick of old-fashioned wheatcakes that everything went black before my eyes, and when I came to— there were crêpes Suzette.

King Edward VII had nothing to do with it.

Artist's Model
Succumbs!

A STRANGE case has just come to light involving an artist's model in London, who, to date, has not been able to drive one man mad. She hasn't been able even to drive one man to drink. The police are working on it now.

Dorine LaBoeuf was the only daughter of a poor laborer, and was born in a thatched hut, or hutched thatch, in Normandy. Or hatched thutch.

She was noted for her beauty, even in those days—which will give you some idea. Later she married and settled down in Lyons and never went to London at all. So, you will see, we have started off with the wrong girl. She has nothing to do with the story at all, and I don't know what I was thinking of.

*　　*　　*　　*　　*

The girl *I* mean was born in Kansas City, but was fatter than Dorine LaBoeuf as a child. She was so fat that they despaired of her life at

one time, but when she got to London (*how
she got to London is another story*—and a better one) she calmed down a little and got a job
as an artist's model. She posed for automobile
accessories and moccasins.

Now, everyone knows that an artist's model
is quite likely to drive men mad, and end up
as a dope feind. (*i* before *e*, except after *c*.)
This girl, in spite of her great beauty and collection of time-tables, couldn't even manage to
end up as a dope fiend. (The proofreader
caught it this time.)

I hope I'm not boring you.

She posed and she posed and she posed, but
nobody ever even threatened to kill *her*, much
less himself. It was the slowest year for suicides
that London had had since Chelsea became the
Greenwich Village of America.

*   *   *   *   *

We are now getting around slowly to the unpleasant fact that this girl was not so hot-look-
ing. *She* thought she was, and the man at the
desk thought she was fair (that's the way he
phrased it: "She's fair") , but that was where it
ended.

I don't know why I'm telling you all this,
except that you asked me to tell you the story

of the London model who didn't drive men mad. You don't remember that, do you? I suppose that next you'll be saying that you aren't even reading this.

Well, all fooling aside now! This girl is actually in London at this minute, and I can prove it. And do you know who she is? She is the wife of a very prominent man, who offered me a great deal of money (three dollars) if I would keep it out of the papers.

But once a newspaperman, always a newspaperman, and a good "story" (newspaper jargon for "cub") is more important than all the money in the world. That's why newspapermen are so poorly paid.

Those Dicta

SCIENTISTS would get a lot farther with me if they didn't generalize so dogmatically. For every general dictum that they issue, at least three exceptions can be found right in my own house.

A Soviet psychologist has come out with one which sends me into paroxysms of rage every time I think about it.

"Brain sensitivity varies with the seasons," he says. "In the Spring the sensitivity of the brain is greatest, which explains why mankind always feels better in the Spring."

"Mankind," eh? Well, I, and at least eight other people that I happen to know, feel lousy in the Spring and top-hole in the Fall, and what do you know about that, you Communistic old doctor, you? Just because *you* happen to feel best in the Spring it turns out that "mankind" feels best in the Spring.

I don't know anything about my brain sensitivity (and, apparently, you don't, either), but I do know that I reach my low point in May

I do know that I reach my low point in May

and am my peppiest in October. And I flatter myself that I am a member of that group which is known, euphemistically, as mankind. Not a member in very good standing, perhaps, but good enough to have a vote on the seasons. And I didn't give you my proxy, either.

Another dictum which makes me see red is the one issued by all scientific analysts of humor, namely that the universal joke, the one thing that all "mankind" thinks is funny, is the sight of some one else slipping on a banana peel and falling. They always use this banana peel as the example, which is a tip-off in itself, on their own range of humor.

Now, I *don't* happen to think that it is funny to see anyone else slip on a banana peel and fall, and I know several other people who don't, either. I don't claim that we are right in this. All that I claim is that it is not the "universal joke." And I'll thank the learned humor-analysts not to go around saying that "everyone" laughs at it, and basing their theories on that premise.

"Mankind feels best in the Spring." "Everyone laughs at a man slipping on a banana peel." "All dreams are based on sex." "Self-preservation is the first law of mankind." With possibly fifty million exceptions.

The trouble with the specialists in what mankind does or does not do is that they don't get around enough with mankind.

The
Vigil

NOT content with saddling me with a blood-thirsty bird, who sits in the tree outside my window and threatens me, the Fates have now visited me with a love-sick dog, who sits day and night on my doorstep and mopes. It is too much.

Up until last week I had, as a house-guest, a very respectable and (I must admit) attractive girl dog, a spaniel of a light mocha hue, who was not without a certain ingenuous flirtatious charm. She made contacts in the neighborhood, and once there were rumors of an engagement.

Nothing came of it, however, and last week her owner, concerned with more mundane matters, took her away to visit the Yosemite, where, I have no doubt, she divides her time between a contemplation of the grandeur of Nature and minor affairs of the heart.

But she has left behind her a very sad and rather elderly spaniel, who sits and sits on every doorstep that I have, waiting for her return. He must belong to someone in the neighborhood, for I remember having seen him for a long time romping about with the other boys. But he romps no longer, and he, apparently, never goes home.

He has large, rheumy eyes, like a nonagenarian and he looks at me as I pass in and out of the house with an accusing stare, as if to say: "What have you done with her, you cad?" I have almost come to believe, myself, that I am responsible for something.

He is not a physically attractive dog. He is on the brown and white side and I think a little too large for a spaniel. From lying about so much on our doorsteps and in the flower beds, he is, by now, quite unkempt.

I have tried shooing him away, rather crossly. I have said to him in so many words: "She is no longer here, my lad. My advice to you would be to forget her. But, even if you cannot forget her, do go home and cease haunting me."

But he doesn't go home. No matter how late I come in (and it was almost midnight last night, I guess, because the sun was coming up) there he is on the doorstep, looking at me with those accusing eyes. It is getting on my nerves. God knows I have done nothing to his girl.

I almost like the bird, now. At least, the bird comes right out with it.

Haircut, Please!

AMONG other things that I am finding it increasingly difficult to get, is a haircut. I just can't seem to bring myself to make the first move.

In my more *soigné* days I had no difficulty in walking right into a barber shop every Tuesday (I chose Tuesday because it is the day that *Variety* comes out) and saying, in ringing tones, "Haircut, please." Those were the days when I was known as "Beau Bob."

But gradually, as my life became more sedentary, I began to find it difficult to leave the house until after the barber shops had closed. Those that were open in the evening somehow didn't have the knack of fixing my peculiar hair-line in back so that I didn't look like a shepherd.

It got to be once every two weeks instead of once every week, and then once every three weeks. Now, for the greater part of each month, I give the impression of having just come from Oberammergau to look for a job. In Holly-

*Those were the days when I was
known as "Beau Bob"*

wood, it is just taken for granted that I am
working in "Mutiny on the Bounty."

* * * * *

Several times I have tried having a barber
come into my place and cut my hair, since it
is obvious that I am never going to be able to
get out to his place. This luxury, however, suf-
fuses me with a sense of decadence, and I feel
that all I need is three or four dancing girls

*I look inside, hoping all the
chairs are occupied*

to bring about the Revolution, with me at the
bottom of the pile. Also, it takes quite a lot of
nerve to call the barber.

The thing has now reached a stage where it
is practically a phobia. When, by some convulsion of Nature, I do find myself in front of a
barber shop in the daytime, I stand and look
inside, hoping that all the chairs are occupied.

If they are not, I sometimes wait until they are. Then I go on my way with an easy conscience.

I guess that the answer is that I shall have to learn to cut my own hair. I am dreading that phase.

The
Flying Flea

THERE are some compensations for being in the middle generation. The chances are that none of us will ever have to operate a "flying flea" in our daily routine.

The "flying flea" is a wingless autogiro which is destined, according to some people whom I do not trust, to be the means of transportation for the business man of the future. (That is, if there is any business in the future.)

In the "flying flea" the pilot can drive along the highway, as in an automobile, until he reaches a field. Up to this point I string along with the inventor. It is after the thing reaches the field that I am wondering about.

"Here he will take off," says the prospectus, "aided by a new jump feature recently perfected. Like a flea, the giro will jump upward from 15 to 25 feet. Then, before it can drop back, the propeller will take hold and normal flight begin."

*　　*　　*　　*　　*

The catch, as I see it, comes in that "before it can drop back." If I know propellers, they are not always sure-fire on the first spin. And, when you are 15 to 25 feet up in the air, the first spin is more or less what counts. There really isn't time to fool around with a second or third.

They should have left the words "before it can drop back" out of the sales talk. They emphasize too strongly the possibility of the Law of Gravitation's having its way with the giro. The propeller may not work the first time, but the Law of Gravitation is usually pretty reliable on the first crack out of the box.

I guess a man would feel pretty silly, after having made a leap like a flea up into the air for 15 or 20 feet, to find that was as far as he was going, and that the return trip to earth was setting in almost immediately. The humiliation alone would be something.

However, being more or less wedded to the bicycle, I expect to be spared any such dispiriting experience with a "flying flea." It is comforting to be sure of something in this unpredictable world.

Phobias

THE discovery of phobias by the psychiatrists has done much to clear the atmosphere. Whereas in the old days a person would say: "Let's get the heck out of here!" today he says: "Let's get the heck out of here! I've got claustrophobia!"

Most everybody knows the name of the phobia that he has personally, and it is a great comfort to him. If he is afraid of high places, he just says: "Oh, it's just my old acrophobia," and jumps.

If he is afraid of being alone he knows that he has monophobia and has the satisfaction of knowing that he is a pathological case. If he keeps worrying, in the middle of a meal, about the possibility of being buried alive, he can flatter himself that he has taphephobia, and that it is no worse than a bad cold.

* * * * *

But there are some honeys among the phobias that don't get much publicity. There is, for example, phobophobia, which is the fear of having a phobia, even though you may not have one at the moment. This takes the form of the patient sitting in terror and saying to himself: "Supposing I should be afraid of food, I would starve to death!" Not a very pretty picture, you will admit.

Then there is kemophobia, or the fear of sitting too close to the edge of a chair and falling off. People with kemophobia are constantly hitching themselves back in their chairs until they tip themselves over backward. This gives the same general effect as falling off the chair frontward, so they find themselves in a *cul-de-sac*.

Then there is goctophobia, or the fear of raising the hand too far and striking oneself in the face, with the possibility of putting an eye out. These patients keep their hands in their pockets all the time and have to be fed by paid attendants. A nasty complication arises when they also have nictophobia, or fear of paid attendants.

* * * * *

Some of the other little known phobias are octophobia, or fear of the figure 8; genophobia, or the fear of being burned on door-handles; kneebophobia, or the fear that one knee is going to bend backwards instead of forwards some day, and optophobia, or the dread of opening the eyes for fear of what they will see.

Tell us your phobias and we will tell you what you are afraid of.

The
Camel Market

THE New South Wales correspondent of
the *International News Service* forwards
the disquieting news that a man named Manning, living in Newcastle, N. S. W., has just
bought a camel at auction for the small sum of
$1.25, or five shillings. There are two ways of
looking at this.

Five shillings is not a good price for a camel,
even though these are not boom days. In fact,
it comes under the head of starvation prices.
The camel market in New South Wales cannot
be glutted. It is more than likely that this was
the only camel in the country. What price Re-
covery if an exclusive camel drags down only
five shillings at an auction?

*   *   *   *   *

On the other hand, the affair has its brighter
side. The camel was the property of the Shire
Council, which had impounded it. (The correspondent doesn't say how it happened to be
there for the Shire Council to impound, but

there may have been a previous story which I didn't catch.) The fact that the camel was put up at auction at all shows that the Shire Council felt that things were picking up in the Newcastle district. They could have just ignored it.

I wish that there had been more about the auction itself. Just what is the selling talk for a camel in New South Wales? How would an auctioneer go about stimulating frantic bidding?

"Gentlemen! Here is a camel!" Then what?

"How much am I bid for this marvelous camel? Denizen of the desert, the Arabian's best friend, sometimes called 'the Crouching Horse of Sandyland!' How much am I bid for this indispensable pet?

* * * * *

"Look at him, gentlemen! Mount him if you wish! . . . No, my good man, not that way—you face *front*—that's right! Is that a mount worth owning? Tell the gentlemen what you see from up there. The ocean? You hear, gentlemen? Mr. Manning says that he can see the ocean from his seat on this camel! Is that something, or isn't it?

"Do I hear four shillings?"

Mr. Manning (from the camel's back): "Four shillings!"

"Fine! Four shillings bid for this exquisite camel! Do I hear five?"

Mr. Manning: "Five shillings!"

"Good! Mr. Manning has bid five shillings against himself! Do I hear six? . . . Going—going—at five shillings—*sold* to Mr. Manning for five shillings!"

Mr. Manning pays his five shillings and rides off.

* * * * *

The next news story we shall look for is the one telling what Mr. Manning did with the camel.

The
Curse Shortage

THE art of cursing people seems to have lost its tang since the old days when a good malediction took four deep breaths to deliver and sent the outfielders scurrying toward the fence to field.

The best we seem able to do nowadays is some sissy cliché like: "May all your children be acrobats!" after which we laugh and buy drinks all around to show that there is really no hard feeling. We just don't seem to care any more whether anyone is properly cursed or not.

*   *   *   *   *

The last real, cellophane-wrapped curse that came to my attention was delivered at the start of the World War by an ardent and zealous Greek patriot, and Eleutherios Venizelos was the lucky boy. The patriot was cross at M. Venizelos because he was pro-Ally, and this is how he showed his irritation:

"Against this traitor Venizelos we have invoked the following injuries: the ulcers of Job, the whale of Jonah, the leprosy of Naaman, the bite of Death, the shivering of the dying, the thunderbolt of Hell and the malediction of God and man."

"And," he might have added, "a bad head cold."

The good man went even farther, caught up in the spirit of the thing. "We shall call for the same injuries upon those who at the coming elections shall vote for the Traitor Venizelos, and we shall further pray for their hands to wither and for them to become deaf and blind."

* * * * *

It was obvious that the patriot was taking sides in the election, or at any rate, had leanings. The funny part of it was that Venizelos won out and, so far as anyone could notice with his clothes on, contracted none of the troubles wished on him, not even the whale of Jonah. He didn't do it so well in his recent revolution, but he looked all right in the news reels. Maybe the curse was on a long-term endowment plan, falling due in 1940.

At any rate we are getting nowhere with our present-day milk-and-water maledictions. Either we ought to wish everybody well or think up some original, four-motored curses. Perhaps the telegraph companies could put their Fathers' Day men to work on it and give us a list to choose from.

First
Aid

NOT being much of a haemophile and being fairly immune against infection
from anything smaller than B-B shot, I do not
keep abreast of the antiseptic procession. Unless
a germ starts trying to wrestle, I usually let him
alone on me. I find that he goes away sooner
or later.

But when the subject of tetanus or sunburn
or medicine chests creeps into a dinner conversation, as it often does just before the salad, I
am appalled at my medieval faith in what seems
to be witches' brews and black magic. All of
my little cure-alls have evidently been discred-
ited as long ago as March, 1935.

*   *   *   *   *

I always take my tip on emergency remedies
from those "in the know." There was a time
when anything that was cut had to be dipped
immediately in, let us say, "Cut-a-Mint." No
first-class medicine cabinet was without "Cut-a-
Mint." So I lay in a stock of "Cut-a-Mint."

302

"Didn't you know that it actually spreads cuts?"

This would be, perhaps, in June. By the following October, some random investigator, looking through my medicine chest for dental floss, would say in horror: "You don't use 'Cut-a-Mint,' do you? Didn't you know that it actually *spreads* cuts? Didn't you read the latest bulletin of the Bleeders' Research Division?"

Well, I have so much Latin to read during the week that I hadn't got around to the bulletin, but I am willing to take any expert advice (which is why 1929 was such a bad financial year for me, having been a, Virgo child), so I would throw away all my "Cut-a-Mint" and lay in a stock of "Hypo-Haemo," the new anti-

303

septic. "They used it all during the War, you know," was the recommendation, and certainly anything that they used all during the War must have been O.K., because the War was a great success.

But by the time I had a chance to use my "Hypo-Haemo" some investigators had got out a report exposing it as nothing but tea with a little developing fluid in it, and the smart ones were off on another tack—just plain chloride of lime with a wintergreen odor. You rub it in.

* * * * *

I have about decided that when I cut myself, or cut anyone else, I will just forget about it and let Nature take its course. I suppose that they have found out something about Nature by now. There is certainly plenty to find out.

No More
Nightmares

THERE is a new treatment for nightmares (I never knew about the old one as a mattee of fact) which involves the use of perfumes, will power and music, any of which you can procure at your dealer's. Just ask for a "nightmare kit."

The nightmare victim lies down on a couch and relaxes—a tough assignment right at the start for a nightmare victim. His face is covered with four layers of gauze, muffling nose, mouth, eyes and ears. So far it looks as if we were on the wrong track.

But, get this! Jasmine and tuberose perfumes are then dropped on the gauze and symphony music is played. If the symphony orchestra happens to be out on tour at the time or you haven't got enough chairs in the house, chamber music will do. Someone could even just hum a symphony, I suppose.

*　　*　　*　　*　　*

The patient then becomes somnolent, according to the prospectus, although what probably happens is that he is smothered into insensibility. He is supposed to run through a routine of day-dreams, carefully selected in advance, retracing the ideals of the patient's youth, such as playing shortstop for the Red Sox or running a canoe rental landing.

He lies in this state for half or three-quarters of an hour, with a soft gong sounding from time to time. (Quite a lot of props are needed for this nightmare cure. It is strictly a rich man's treatment.) The gong is the signal to change dreams. No matter where you are in the action of one day-dream you change to another when the gong sounds. This, I should think, would cause neurasthenia and general debility, but I guess the doctors know best.

One of the changes is the conscious introduction of the nightmare itself. The patient forces his imagination to go through with the nightmare, daring it to do its worst. The jasmine and tuberose are, in the meantime, getting in their work, but the symphony orchestra has knocked off at five and gone home.

* * * * *

This treatment is not only for bad dreams,

but "depression insomnias, anxiety, moderate stupors and confusion." I'll take a book of ten tickets for treatments for confusion, please, with an extra hour on Saturdays for a moderate stupor.

Ominous
Announcements

TO THE man who has been out late the night before, or even to just the nervous man who winces at unusual commotions, there is no more upsetting announcement than: "The expressmen are here for the trunks!"

Better never go away for the Summer than face the arrival of the expressmen for the trunks on a jumpy morning. It isn't so much what the expressmen do *after* they get into the room. It is the shock of the announcement that they are downstairs and on their way up! It is like seeing a comet rushing toward the earth at a million miles a second.

* * * * *

In the first place, the trunks are very likely not quite ready, which makes for confusion, and confusion is just the thing you do not want on that particular morning. "Above all things, no confusion!" you have said, as you agreed to get up out of bed that morning. "No confusion, and a minimum of crashing about, please!" And here are the expressmen!

"The express men are here for the trunks!"

Then the trunks always seem to be too heavy for the helpers. They must run across some pretty heavy trunks in their day's work and, after all, it *is* their work and they knew what it was going to be like when they went into it, but yours is evidently more than even an expressman's helper could be expected to face. What have you got in it—rocks?

This attitude on their part does not help you in your own mental strain. You feel every tug on their muscles, as if it were on your own, and the sweat starts from your own forehead as they finally grunt their way out of the room, neatly chipping off a large segment from the door-

*Strange faces peering out
from the bathroom can be
pretty frightening*

jamb. It would have been simpler to have car
ried the trunk down yourself.

* * * * *

Another announcement of almost equal im-
plications to the man who dreads disruption
of the regular, easy flow of household life is:
"The plumber's here to fix the bathroom!"

He couldn't wait until afternoon, when you
might be feeling better. Oh, no! He must come
at crack of dawn, with all his instruments and
blow-torches, like a fiend from hell. The water
must be shut off, pipes must be hammered and
banged, and, above all, strangers will be poking

their heads in and out of doors where you are accustomed to seeing only familiar faces.

Strange faces peering out from the bathroom can be pretty frightening if you are not in good health or spirits.

* * * * *

On the whole, it is better for the man who craves the Old Order of Things on any particular morning to go down in the cellar and sit. Then, probably, he will hear from the head of the stairs: "The man's here to fix the hot-water heater!"

"East, West, Home's Best!"

IN CASE your house or apartment has begun to pall on you and you are getting sick of the same old molding and the same old windows every day, just notify an agent that he may bring people around to look the place over for rental. You'll want to stay then, just out of spite.

People who are doing what is known as "looking at" an apartment are unpleasant people in the very nature of things. They are passing judgment on a place in which you have, for better or for worse, been living for some time. There's an insult, right there.

In the first place they always come "to look" when you are in your bare feet, or have half your face covered with lather. You may have thought that you kept the place fairly tidy, but the minute the "lookers" come in the door it takes on, even in your eyes, the appearance of a house in one of William Faulkner's novels, where poor mountain-whites have been inbreeding and cooking pork chops for genera-

It's those glances that get your
back up

tions. You can tell that it wouldn't surprise
them to see an old sheep stagger out of a corner.

*   *   *   *   *

Then they begin. You try to pay no attention
and to give them the run of the place by themselves, but you hear them whispering, or see
them exchange glances. It's those glances that
get your back up. Whatever you may pretend
to be doing while they are looking (and it usually is something spurious, like winding your
watch or patting down sofa cushions which don't
need patting) you are burning up as you go
through the motions.

"I suppose this is the dining-room," the woman says. (She *supposes* it is the dining room! It's got a dining-room table and chairs and a sideboard in it, hasn't it? What does she want—a steaming roast ox spread out for her?)

"It's not very light, is it?" (It's light enough for *you*, old girl! You can stand a few shadows, with that pan!)

"It might be a little more cheerful with other curtains." (One of the reasons you want to leave may have been the dark dining room, but it now seems like a sun parlor to you. Other curtains, indeed!)

* * * * *

Then they pass on into the kitchen, where they think they are out of earshot.

"Helma would never work here, I know." (And who is Helma to refuse to work in *your* kitchen? Better cooks than Helma have managed to whip themselves into working there.)

Then you hear an "Ugh!" No remark—just an "Ugh!" There certainly is nothing in that kitchen to go "Ugh!" about, unless she has got into the icebox and doesn't like cold beets. She'd better get out of that icebox or you'll

Then you hear an "ugh!"

have the police on her. She's not renting cold beets from you. She's not renting anything from you, if you have your way. You're going to stay right there yourself.

As they come back surprising you at your pillow patting you ask if they want to have you show them the bedrooms. The woman smiles a nasty smile and says no, they won't put you to that trouble, as they have almost decided (*an exchange of glances*) that the place is not quite large enough for them. They have a little girl, you see. Well, it must be a pretty big little girl

to crowd them, in a place this size. Pretty big,
and pretty disagreeable.

*   *   *   *   *

So they leave, with polite thanks, which do
not fool you for a minute, and you come back
into the dear little nest that you call Home,
and that you are going to call Home for at least
another year, God willing.

But you do take a little look into the kitchen
to see what that "Ugh!" was for.

No More
Bananas

IT IS perhaps presumptuous for any one of us to say just what he will or will not do with the remaining days allotted to him, but I think that I may safely predict this: I am off bananas, definitely.

More in the nature of a whim than anything else (I really don't need to take off *much* weight —possibly ten or twelve pounds here and there, now that the bathing suit season is coming on), I started last week on what is known as the "banana and skimmed milk diet," or the Johns Hopkins glide. I am no longer on it, but, even after a three days' work-out, I swear that if a banana so much as crosses my path, I will shoot it down like a dog.

As I understood it, you took two bananas and a glass of skimmed milk three times a day for two weeks. Then you bought yourself a white mess-jacket and a wide black sash, and chased Clifton Webb for the concavity prize. That was what I heard.

*   *   *   *   *

*To make things harder,
I never liked bananas
much anyway*

I started on a Monday morning with my two bananas and a glass of skimmed milk. To make things harder, I never liked bananas very much, anyway. Two-thirds of the way down even one banana I am willing to concede defeat smilingly and give the rest to the nearest monkey. Here were *two* bananas. And two more for lunch. And two more for dinner. I began to look upon the skimmed milk as more or less of a cordial. Then my friends began:

"It isn't two bananas three times a day; it's three bananas twice a day. I read it in a medical journal."

"You're crazy to do it that way. You are supposed to stay in bed the whole two weeks and have the bananas rubbed into your arm."

"Bananas and skimmed milk! You know what

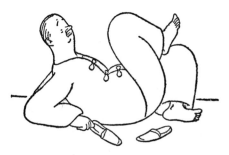

*I fell down while trying to get into
my slippers*

that'll do to you, don't you? Just turn your
liver to rubber, that's all!"

"I know of a girl who tried that diet, and,
when they cut her open, they found that she
was all coated over inside with banana oil."

"I hope you're sure that the bananas are not
too hard. The action of milk on hard bananas
when they get in your stomach together—well,
go ahead with it if you want to."

*　　*　　*　　*　　*

Now, all this time I was none too happy as
it was, without outside heckling on the subject.
I began cutting my bananas up into cubes for
one meal, into diamonds for the next, and
finally I mashed them up with the milk into a
cocktail shaker and gave myself quite a party.
That was the evening of the second day.

319

It was on the third day that I decided to call the whole thing off. I got up in the morning and fell down while trying to get into my slippers. As I ate my three-and-a-half-minute bananas, with a dash of Worcestershire on them, and drank my cup of steaming hot skimmed milk (dated), I glanced over the morning paper:

HULL AND WALLACE ARGUE BANANA BILL WITH REPUBLICANS.

PAY CUT RESTORED TO BANANA LABOR.

BANANA KIDNAPERS SURROUNDED IN ARIZONA.

10,000 BANANAS IN GERMANY DEFY NAZI EDICT.

Such were the headlines that greeted my eye. I put my paper down. "Juliette," I called out as loudly as my enfeebled condition would allow, "a plate of ham and eggs, wheat cakes and coffee, *with* cream! And if you have any of the roast pork left over from last night, put a piece on the plate with the muffins. I want to wrap it up in a banana-skin and take it to the office for my lunch."

*   *   *   *   *

And that, kiddikins, is why you must never mention bananas in front of Grandpa if you don't want a good, swift clout across your pretty little mouths.

You
Mr. Grown-Up!

ONE of the eight things which are supposed to be wrong with the present generation of adults (not including the mere fact of *being* in the present generation of adults, which is no small handicap in itself) is that we didn't learn enough about the science of physics when we were young. Well, it might as well be that as anything.

All of this is being remedied in the coming generation, thanks to the model laboratories where children are being taught to do little tricks which involve the principle of light refraction and the coefficient of linear expansion. The best of it is that they don't know that they are being taught anything. They just think they're playing with eggs and matches.

* * * * *

Here is a list of problems which any kiddie in the modern laboratory can do. It is printed in the paper under the heading: "Mr. Grown-Up, Can You Do These Things?" Well, "Mr.

Grown-Up" isn't my name, in the first place. And I *can* do these things, in the second. I may mess things up a little, but I'll get them done somehow. No child of six is going to get ahead of me.

1. Can you place a shelled, hard-boiled egg in the mouth of a milk bottle, and, without touching it, cause it to plop into the bottle?

Sure I can. I haven't figured it out yet, but I'll do it if I have to use a robin's egg. (Ha-ha —you hadn't thought of that, had you, Mr. Six-Year-Old?)

2. Tell why a stick, placed in water at an angle, appears to be bent at the surface.

What makes you think it does? (That's telling 'em, eh, Fat Lady?)

3. Produce a series of sounds like chimes with a piece of string and a teaspoon.

Hit the teaspoon repeatedly with the piece of string until it does give off a series of sounds like chimes. This is just a matter of perseverance. It may take quite a while, but before long you'll kid yourself into thinking you hear chimes, whether you do or not. What's so great about chimes, anyway?

4. Make innumerable images of one object with two mirrors.

That's easy.

5. *Tell why a balloon, only partly inflated, will apparently fill up when held tightly over the top of a milk bottle filled with steam.*

Because it *does* fill up. You didn't expect me to fall backward at that one, did you?

6. *Make a lighted candle seem to be burning inside a glass of water.*

Place the candle inside the glass of water and light it.

*   *   *   *   *

Well, that cleans up Mr. Grown-Up's part of the examination. Now we'll ask Mr. Six-Year-Old some questions.

Sluggards, Ahoy!

A T A recent so-called "hobby exhibit" in New York a young man entered as his hobby a colony of ants. I remember thinking at the time: "Well, sir ——"

Presumably the young man, who was specializing in zoology, took up ants as a hobby because he subscribed to the age-old theory that Man has a great deal to learn from the ants. As a matter of fact the only thing that I ever learned from an ant was not to try to carry too big a crumb on my back or I would walk sideways.

And now along comes as smart an ant-watcher as Professor Julian Huxley, who says that we humans can not only hold our own with ants, but possibly might be able to slip over a couple of tricks on them once in a while.

* * * * *

"One of the important differences between a human being and a termite is the matter of size," says Professor Huxley, cracking down with a dictum. "*Important* difference," Professor? It's colossal! It's the difference between my sleeping in my bed or an ant's sleeping there, that's all.

"If we had ants as big as fox terriers and wasps as big as eagles," continues Dr. Huxley —but there I left him. I don't want to know what the end of that sentence was. And I don't want anyone ever to begin a sentence that way again, either—at least, not within my hearing.

The comforting thing about Prof. Huxley's lecture was the statement that we really don't have to learn anything from the ant. We can go our way and the ant can go his. Contrary to our teachings, we do not have to be bending over all the time studying how the ants do it.

*   *   *   *   *

Human beings and ants have a great many things in common, however. They are the only organisms which have rubbish heaps, slaves and domestic animals, and which make war with military precision. Which brings me to a remark of Mrs. Patrick Campbell's, as what doesn't?

Mrs. Campbell was sitting at dinner next to an ant-watcher, who was telling, at considerable length, about the remarkable organization of ant communities.

"They have teams and working units, with sub-divisions of labor," he said. "An ant community even has an army."

"No navy, I suppose?" asked Mrs. Campbell.

Which just about fixes the ants.

Sweet
Solitude

EVERY man owes it to himself (and his friends) to get away entirely alone in an isolated shack every so often, if only to find out just what bad company he can be.

I don't mean just getting upstairs alone for an evening and reading bound volumes of *Harper's Weekly* without answering the telephone. There's quite a lot of kick in that, and one ought to come downstairs the next morning a better man.

What I mean is an isolation that would make Thoreau on Walden Pond look like a bookmaker at a racetrack. I mean to have somebody drive you out to a shack on a sand dune and then drive off without you, calling back, "See you Thursday!" Let's see—Saturday, Sunday, Monday, Tuesday, Wednesday, Thursday— Hey, Eddie—come back!

* * * * *

Here's the thing you always thought you'd like to do—get away from it all! Just settle down absolutely alone by yourself and check up. Take my advice and *don't ever check up!* Take my advice and settle down right in the middle of Piccadilly Circus with a good book.

The first thing you do is to go around front and take a look at the ocean. That's a big ocean all right. Just a shade *too* big, if you ask me. Now go around back and look at the moors. Yes, sir—there are the moors! Now what?

Well, you might as well start in on that bag of books you brought. You wanted to catch up on your reading. All right, *catch* up on it! Go ahead—*catch* up! You're so fond of reading—go ahead, read a book.

* * * * *

Let's see, the rest of Saturday, all of Sunday, Monday, Tuesday. Don't go on that way, or you'll go crazy. Maybe you'll go crazy anyway. Maybe you were crazy before, and now you're going sane. Maybe that's the top of your head flying off—or was it just a gull going by? Suppose it were a gull *with* the top of your head! What about a good, loud scream?

You could scramble yourself some eggs. That's a good idea, even if it is only four o'clock in the afternoon. It's something to do, at any rate. Scrambled eggs—ambled screggs—drangled geggs—smammbled mreggs—grambled smeggs. So *this* is the mind which God gave you to work things out with! This is called "communing with yourself"!

Heigh-ho! Eggs over! My, my—here it is a quarter to five of a Saturday (Sunday, Monday, Tuesday, Wednesday, *Thursday*) afternoon. Almost bedtime. Why not? You're here for a rest. Sleep, they say, knits up the raveled sleeve of care, the death of each day's life, sore Labour's bath, balm of hurt minds, great Nature's second course, chief nourisher in life's feast. Not bad!

*   *   *   *   *

Now would be a good time to think. Think about what? There must be lots of things to think about. Name *one*! Life. . . . All right, think about Life, you're so crazy about thinking. . . . I guess that *was* the top of your head that gull had. . . . And will he be sore when he finds out that it isn't a fish!

Bed at five-thirty . . . eight good hours of sleep, and up with a bound at one-thirty A. M. eady for another day! Anyway, it's Sunday. Monday, Tuesday, Wednesday, *Thursday*! How about scrambling some eggs? Scrambled eggs—

ambled screggs . . . come, come! No more of *that*!

*　*　*　*　*

A look at the ocean . . . a look at the moors . . . a look at the bag of books . . . a look at yourself in the mirror . . . Boo! You pretty thing! See how far you can stick your tongue out. . . . See if you can raise one eyebrow and lower the other. . . . See if you can look like Bismarck. . . . You *are* Bismarck! . . . Hi-ya, Bismarck!

(Editor's Note: This fragment of manuscript was found floating in a bather off Santa Barbara.)

Penguin Feud

THERE is bad news from the Toledo (Ohio) Zoo. Admiral and Jake, the two penguin buddies, have had a falling out. They don't speak.

Admiral and Jake were recently acquired from the South Polar regions, where they were popular favorites and, according to South Polar gossip, inseparable. They even insisted that they be booked together at the Toledo Zoo, for, as Admiral said when approached for the engagement: "Jake and I are like that!"

On arriving in Toledo they were put in the same pen (at their request), and when Admiral went into the pool for his morning-noon-afternoon-and-evening dip Jake went, too. Sometimes it was Jake who went first, with Admiral following. (We mustn't give you the idea that Jake was just the weakling of the combination. The two were equally interested in each other.)

*　*　*　*　*

I am taking this all on the word of the Zoo

authorities, but it is also said that Admiral and Jake took strolls together around the pen and discussed the latest news from the South Polar regions in a temperate, though definitely intimate, manner. So far as the police can learn, there was never a sign of personal animosity, never a harsh word or an ugly look. There was even some idea of changing their names to Damon and Pythias.

Then—like a bolt from the blue—something happened! Whether it was something that Admiral said, or something that Jake didn't say, no one will ever know. The fact remains that the other day they definitely severed relations. No brawling, you understand. Just an agreement to disagree.

Admiral now takes his plunge alone, and Jake waits until he is through. Jake totters back and forth on his constitutional, and Admiral watches from his club window until Jake has finished and then whips out for a brisk walk alone. If they happen to meet they look the other way. Jake bows slightly.

*   *   *   *   *

I took the liberty of interviewing them for my paper, but I must confess that I could get nothing from either one. Both being Harvard men, they preferred to let the matter go without publicity. After all, what concern is it of the outside world?

I quote Jake first: "There is really nothing in the story at all. Admiral and I are still great friends. It is true that we do not see each other as much as we did, but what of that? I am sure that I speak for Admiral as well as for myself when I say that, should the occasion arise for a joint effort in behalf of some common cause, I would gladly coöperate—to the extent of tending my name with his."

Admiral was perhaps more personal: "Jake is—or was—too good a friend of mine for me to imply that the reason for our split-up was due to his insufferable curiosity. 'What are you doing tonight?' 'Who was that you were talking to?' 'Where did you get that fish?' I simply could not stand it, that's all! But please do not print anything that would hurt Jake. I am sure that things will be straightened out, and that we shall be back together again before long. I mean too much to Jake for him to let me go."

*   *   *   *   *

When shown the above statement of Admiral's, Jake merely said: "That's what *he* thinks!"

In the meantime, the officials of the Toledo Zoo are in a quandary. Should they put Admiral and Jake in two separate pens or just let them work it out for themselves? Sometimes these things go on for months, and, after all, Admiral and Jake were hired as a team.

Coffee
Versus Gin

WHAT is it with these people at Cornell and other hotbeds of medical research that they are always monkeying around with experiments on liquor? They are always trying to find out how many cubic centimeters of alcohol you can take before the salivary glands start drying up, or how much black coffee it takes to counteract the effects of a shot of gin. What do you *care?*

Presumably drinking is a carefree occupation; at any rate while you are drinking. If it isn't a lark, it certainly isn't anything else. It certainly isn't practical; we know that. I don't suppose you would find one man in a hundred who has made a nickel by taking a drink.

So why all this "cubic centimeter" talk? Why go at it so hard-headedly? Why drag in the salivary glands? *We* know they dry up. You don't have to work in a Cornell laboratory to know that.

*   *   *   *   *

It has never kept me awake yet

The particular experiments which have thrown me into such a fever-heat of indignation had to do with the use of coffee as an antidote for liquor. Seventy-five cubic centimeters of gin followed immediately by ten grams of coffee in a half pint of water and the gin had no effect. I've got a better scheme than that. Don't take the seventy-five centimeters of gin at all. Think of all the coffee you'd save!

And, incidentally, I consider coffee greatly overrated as a stimulant. It has never kept me awake yet and it has never started me off with a bang in the morning. A lot of people say: "I'm no good in the morning until I've had my coffee." I'm no good in the morning even *after* I've had my coffee.

This old-wives' superstition that a cup of black coffee will "put you on your feet" with a hangover is either propaganda by the coffee people or the work of dilettante drinkers who get giddy on cooking-sherry. A man with a *real* hangover is in no mood to be told "Just take a cup of black coffee" or "The thing for you is a couple of aspirin." A real hangover is nothing to try out family remedies on. The only cure for a real hangover is death.

* * * * *

On such rare occasions as I feel called upon to work late at night, a cup of black coffee taken at midnight acts as an instantaneous soporific. Two cups and I oversleep in the morning. I like coffee, but it soothes me. And that is one thing I don't need—soothing.

The same people who tell you that a cup of black coffee will put you "on your feet" are also the ones who go around recommending a "good dose of castor oil" for a broken leg. (Why must it always be a *good* dose of castor oil? There is no such thing as a "good" dose of castor oil.) They tell you how to cure hiccoughs, and swear by a glass of hot milk in cases of insomnia. They are nice, kindly people, but you will usually find that they lead fairly sheltered lives. They don't get around much in real suffering circles.

And Cornell or no Cornell, I still don't believe that ten grams of coffee in a half pint of water will offset seventy-five cubic centimeters of gin. How much is seventy-five cubic centimeters of gin, anyway?

The
Early Worm

EARLY rising has several points in its favor,
such as getting first crack at the bathroom
and the best of the coffee brew, but it is likely
to lead to melancholia if you happen to be with
a week-end group of late sleepers. One can roam
about alone just so long, and then madness
sets in.

The man who finds himself, either because
of abundant health or an uncomfortable bed,
up early in the morning on a house-party or
boat trip, is at first suffused with a glow of
superiority. If he is in a position to take a swim
alone in the crisp morning air he becomes well-
nigh insufferable, or would be if there were
anyone awake to suffer from his manner.

*   *   *   *   *

Then comes the tough part. He tiptoes
around, listening at the various doors to find
out if anyone else is awake. Gad! how can people sleep like that! There is nothing so brutish
as someone asleep when you are up and bathed

340

Is at first suffused with a glow of superiority

and coffeed. It shakes one's respect for human nature, that's what it does.

Waking people up deliberately is a little drastic, but there are other ways of disturbing their slumber so that possibly they may awaken by themselves. Stumbling over chairs, playing the radio, or even a well-spotted coughing spell have been known to accomplish this, but you can't count on it. Usually the best you can get is the weak satisfaction of hearing someone roll over.

* * * * *

He tiptoes around listen-
ing at the various doors

There are always four or five books on a shelf
in a beach-house or sailboat, but somehow they
never seem to fit in with a 9 A.M. mood. *The
Golden Ostrich, Lost Heritage, Lady Alice's
Compact* and *Modern Clipper Ships*, all of them
looking as if they had, at some time, been
dipped in brine, usually constitute the lay-out,
with possibly a copy of last week's *New Yorker*
with the cover torn off.

Then it is when brooding sets in. You have
no right to be off on this junket, anyway, with

all that work to do at home. The office may be calling for you at this very minute. The house may be on fire. Your embezzlement may have been discovered. What are you making of your life, anyway?

Pacing up and down, smoking innumerable cigarettes, shadow boxing—none of these expedients serve to calm you. But they wear you out, so that by the time the other members of the party have come peering out for breakfast you are overcome with a belated drowsiness and sleep like a tired child during whatever excitement may follow.

Truffle
Poisoning

ONE of the easiest forms of pretense to break down is the pretense of enthusiasm for exotic foods. Just bring on the exotic foods.

When a man opens his eyes very wide and says, "Boy, what I couldn't do to a rasher of Japanese rollmops right now!" get him a rasher of Japanese rollmops and see what he does to them. The chances are that he can't gag down more than three mouthfuls.

Almost everyone has some little dish that he talks a lot about liking, because it is either hard to get or hard to swallow. But when they are confronted with their dream dish, it very often turns out that nausea flies in the window.

*   *   *   *   *

I used to rave a lot about truffles. (Incidentally, while raving, I mispronounced the word.) Now, all that I actually knew about truffles was that they came as a fixing to several very tasty dishes. I had never really tasted a truffle on the hoof, but I had read about them,

344

*I had to look as much like an
ecstatic epicure as I could*

and talked as if all Paris knew of my craving
for them.

Then, one night, I had my bluff called. A
friend, with whom I was dining, said: "You
ought to be very happy tonight. I see that they
have truffles *au nature* on the menu." I said:
"Oh, boy!"

There being very few things that I cannot
eat with relish, I had every reason to believe
that I could carry on with a truffle, even though
I had never tasted one.

* * * * *

And I probably could have made a go of it
if I had been in top form that night. But I was
more in the mood to be pampered, and a plain
truffle, although considered a delicacy, is not
exactly succulent. It turned out to be some-

345

thing on the order of edible pumice, or a small, black sponge. It had no sauce. Just the pumice.

But I had to dig in and look as much like an ecstatic epicure as I could, smacking my lips and making French gestures with my free hand, while my companion watched with what I thought I detected to be high glee.

I was cured of my truffle talk, but I still have several dishes that I pretend to crave and which I hope I never have to eat under close scrutiny. One of them is *tête de veau,* or the head of a calf served with the brains, ears and eyes.

If you ever hear me raving about *tête de veau,* it will pay you to order me one and watch.

My
Untold Story

CHAPTER I

FOR the benefit of those who are not following the startling "untold stories" of the
down-fall of gun molls, scarlet women and
other celebrities they are currently unfolding in the newspapers, I will give a brief re-
sume of my own untold story, telling, in every
sordid detail, of how I came to New York, an
innocent young man from New England, and
couldn't get myself seduced, even into taking
a glass of beer, for love nor money.

I arrived in New York (for my second try
at it) on New Year's Day, 1916. How memo-
rable that day turned out to be in my life may
be judged from the fact that I just had to look
it up. I would have said that it was 1917.

I was inexperienced in the ways of the world,
being only twenty-six at the time and having
seen nothing of life except that in a very tough
preparatory school, four years in a college notorious for its high living, and a few more years

knocking about in a chain of New England mills. I had also worked for a year in New York, before.

*   *   *   *   *

So, you will see, New Year's Day, 1916, found me wide-eyed and innocent, although I had heard that New York was full of pitfalls for young men like me. I remember asking the policeman, just outside the Grand Central Terminal where I could find the nearest pitfall. He told me that, it being a legal holiday, the pitfalls were all closed.

I neither drank nor smoked, and my experience with women was limited to being married and having one child. But I had heard that, in New York, I should probably be forced to drink if I wanted to keep up with the fast social set of the day. I was prepared, however, to put up a stiff fight.

Being a reporter on a daily newspaper ("the worst reporter, even for his age, in New York," was the affectionate epithet applied to me), I was immediately plunged into the gay life of a newspaper office and the clubs that went with it. Here I met such well-known bon-vivants of the day as Franklin P. Adams, Charles Hansom

348

Towne, Deems Taylor, Arthur Folwell, Izzy Kaplan, Irwin Edman—none of whom drank.

* * * * *

I shall never forget my first "party" in the famous "Tower Room" of Franklin P. Adams, in the old *World* building. The room had been designed by the International Pulp and Paper Company, and was a veritable bower of copy-paper, spittoons and wall calendars for 1914. I knew, when "Frank," as he was called, invited me, that I was about to see life at last. Poor little me!

Some of the fellows had already assembled, Folwell, Taylor, Edman and Kaplan, and soon the cry was: "Everybody over to Dewey's for lunch." Dewey's was a down-town restaurant, famous at that time for its freshly made grape juice. They pressed the grapes right in the window and you could go in and drink your fill. And you may be sure that we all did!

I was a little disappointed at not being offered any hard liquor so that I could refuse it, but the grape juice and steamed cod were so delicious that I soon forgot my little worries and joined in with the rest. It was soon time to go back to the paper to work, where I was assigned to "cover" a banquet of the New Hamp-

349

shire Society, which was being held that evening at the old Waldorf-Astoria! It was my first big assignment!

CHAPTER II

ON BEING told that I was no longer a reporter on the *Tribune* (that would be the old *Tribune*, introduced by P. T. Barnum into this country with great success at Castle Garden, now the Aquarium) I was in a quandary, as you may well imagine. I had been two years in New York, associating with a group of men who were, for the most part, teetotallers, and I had not even learned to drink. Neither could I inhale very well.

I didn't tell Mama that I had lost my job, as Mama was up in New England, and I had no one to go to with my troubles except several wealthy men who had offered to lend me money. I hated to accept money from men, however, as you know how that looks when it comes out in the papers at the trial. So I compromised by borrowing a hundred from one, two hundred from another, and fifty cents from a third. I shall never forget their kindness.

*   *   *   *   *

Fortunately for me, one of them also got me a position as press-agent which paid twice as much as my old newspaper job had paid and threw me at once into the maelstrom of theatrical life on Broadway. Here, at last, it looked as if my dreams of being seduced into some form of wickedness were coming true. You know that theatrical crowd in New York! Hot dickety!

If I were to list all the famous people I met in my life in the theatre, you wouldn't believe me. William A. Brady (my employer); Mrs. William A. Brady (Grace George); A. O. Brown (at that time manager of the Playhouse); Charlie, the carriage-starter; Miss Healy; Julius Cohen (at that time representative of the theatrical advertising agency, now dramatic critic of the *New York Journal of Commerce*); and Lionel Atwill. Here was life with a vengeance for poor little me!

I told Mama that I was working for the B. R. T., as I didn't want her to worry. To this day she doesn't know that I was in the employ of a theatrical producer. Neither does the theatrical producer.

*   *   *   *   *

My office was on the top floor of the Playhouse in the famous "Tower Room." Here I sat all day, amid piles and piles of old newspapers and photographs of road companies of Mr. Brady's *Way Down East*, and typed out stories about how Bernstein came to write *L'Elevation*, the play which Miss George was doing at that time. I also wrote some stories about *The Man Who Came Back*, which was then on the road. The theatre was "getting me," I could tell that.

They didn't like to have me backstage much, but I used to hang around the box-office quite a bit, as I felt that there I was getting a little closer to the smell of grease paint and "the world of make-believe." Mr. Brown was also very good company, and I had no one to talk to up in the famous "Tower Room."

At last, however, Mr. Brown's patience wore out, as the box-office was very small, and, finally, on one matinee day, he asked me why I didn't get out of the way. I had no good answer to this, so I went over to the Capehart Theatrical Advertising Agency and talked with Julius Cohen for a little while.

*   *   *   *   *

I think that Mr. Brown regretted his brusqueness a little, for he was really very kind-hearted, and one Saturday night he said to me.

smiling: "The show closes next Saturday night. You close tonight!"

So that ended my Broadway career for a while, and still I had not been seduced. In all my stay among "the white lights" (two months) I had spoken to only one woman, Miss Healy, up in the office. She was very nice. As Miss George was always very busy, I had met no actresses.

So far, New York had not got its talons into me.

CHAPTER III

AS I walked out of the Playhouse that cold November night, a discharged press-agent, I realized that I was not only broke but, what was worse, unsullied. Neither Newspaper Row nor the Gay White Way had even lifted a finger to drag me down. What was the matter with me, anyway? Wasn't I pretty enough?

But around the corner lay the grim spectre of army life, which has been the downfall of so many young men. My turn was coming, although I did not know it. When I think, that, on that November night of 1917, I had been able neither to get myself lured into taking a drink nor into any wild orgies with women, I smile a wry smile. For, by the end of the war, I had been no more successful.

* * * * *

Having been, at the time of the draft, the father of an exceptionally dependent child, I was placed in what was known as "Class 1-A," or the Sitting Pretty Group. However, it was an imminent necessity for me to get a job of some kind in order to keep a family alive; so a good friend (who shall be nameless, as I have forgotten his name) got me a position (civilian) in Washington, with the Aircraft Board. So, packing up milk containers and diapers, we marched away from the Great City which had failed so miserably as a Hell Hole.

My field headquarters during the war were in Room 911 of the Munsey Building, Washington, D. C., in the very heart of the district which presented so many pitfalls to the young man on leave. On one corner was the New Willard Hotel, with no bar, and on another corner the Capitol Lunch, where egg sandwiches at all hours of the day and night were a constant temptation. The trolley ride out to Chevy Chase each evening was also a rather riotous experience.

354

The Aircraft Board having been given quite a bit of publicity about airplanes which seem never to have been shipped to France, my job was to keep all mention of airplanes out of papers until the affair had blown over. So I sat in Room 911 all day and read all the papers in the United States. It was gruelling work, and sometimes I would come into my office with my shoes caked with the red mud in which our Chevy Chase house was built, but I never whimpered, if I do say so myself. I was waiting for someone to offer me a drink, so that my morale could crack. But no one ever did, darn it!

* * * * *

Among the famous war characters who didn't offer me a drink or suggest that I step out with *mademoiselles* were Mr. Payne and Mr. Horton, who worked in the Aircraft Board office; Mr. Howard Coffin, the chairman (who once inveigled me up to his house for tea, which turned out to be tea), and the Washington newspaper correspondents, who wouldn't have given me a drink if they had had one. I also once talked to a man in uniform, but, as he was a major-general, he said nothing about sin.

So there was poor little Me, having been

through the mill of newspaper work, theatrical work, and war work, and still as virginal in the ways of the world as when I left Mama in Worcester. I was, frankly, discouraged. Was I never to see Life?

CHAPTER IV

AS YOU may well imagine, I was, by this time, a pretty discouraged boy at my vain attempts to taste even a dreg of life. When a boy reaches the age of thirty without having had even a glass of beer or a sly wink from a pair of roguish eyes, things begin to look pretty black for his career as a man-about-town.

So it was with high excitement that I made my first trip to Hollywood, the Sin Capital of the World. "Here it comes at last!" I giggled to myself. "Life in the raw, and then down-down-down!" I could hardly wait.

I shall never forget my first night in Hollywood. I had taken a room at a hotel, and with me was Marc Connelly, a tea merchant, who had knocked around the world quite a bit, and George Jessel, a romantic actor of that period (1926). We had dined wisely, but not very well, and were in the mood for about three-quarters of an orgy. The only trouble was that we were all just a little sleepy. At first, that California air gets you that way.

*   *   *   *   *

Mr. Jessel said that he knew a beautiful girl that he would call up. "We'll have a million laughs," he said. A million laughs wasn't my idea of what constituted a Hollywood orgy, but I figured it out that everyone didn't necessarily have to laugh all the time.

He called the number of the beautiful girl, and while he was waiting he reassured us again. "She's the most beautiful girl you ever saw," he said. Then, after a long wait, he added, "She's so beautiful she isn't at home!"

So he called another number, that of a well-known movie actress. My heart went like a tack-hammer! A movie actress! She turned out to be at home, but just about to go to bed. "On the set at nine tomorrow, you know," she said.

While George called some other actresses' numbers, Marc and I tried to see who could recall the oldest popular song. It was great fun! Then, all of George's numbers being either out or on the point of going to bed, we hit upon a great plan for the rest of the evening.

"Let's go over to Henry's and get an egg sandwich!" said Marc. Like a flash we were off, and ten o'clock saw us in the middle of our second egg sandwich, washed down with an equal number of beakers of milk. (Henry's was the only place in Hollywood that stayed open after nine-thirty, so we were in great good luck to find it.)

And so it went during my whole stay in the Movie Capital. Work all day with Ray Griffiths, who didn't drink and who kept bachelor quarters at the Los Angeles Athletic Club ("open house," we called it), dinner at six-thirty and bed at nine-thirty, reading last Thursday's New York paper from cover to cover. I gained eleven pounds and forgot how to inhale cigarets. (It is a funny thing, but, once I had lost the knack of inhaling, I lost interest in cigarets, and have never smoked them since.)

* * * * *

I met lots of movie actors and actresses, but I guess that I got into the wrong set, for they were all crazy about tennis and early rising. The nearest I got to temptation was once when I went out of the movie colony to Santa Barbara to be best man at Donald Ogden Stewart's wedding and got water on the knee. But I did that all by myself. Nobody tempted me.

Sometimes now I think of those quiet evenings in Hollywood under the reading lamp and wonder if it wouldn't be better if I had stayed there among the orange juice.

CHAPTER V

PARIS! What magic lies in those words!

I could hardly sleep on my first day in Paris, but, as there was nothing much else to do, I turned in at about three in the afternoon, shortly after the arrival of the boat-train, and managed to tear off about fifteen hours. (It had been a very rough crossing, during which I had met no interesting people, and I was dead tired.)

The next morning the sun rose gray and foggy, and I put in a long-distance call for America, just to talk with Mama. (Mama had not come along on the trip, being no fool.)

Then—what to do? The Galleries Lafayette, Cook's, the American Express, all these were names to conjure with. So I conjured with them for a while and then went out for a walk. This broke up the day nicely, especially as it began to rain, and I had to run for it, I can tell you. As our hotel was on a side street, through which no one had passed since the days of the Commune, I, fortunately, had plenty of room in which to run. But was I out of breath! Hot-dickety!

*　　*　　*　　*　　*

That evening I was all agog, except for my dress tie, which I had lost somewhere. We were going to the Folies Bergères! Here anything might happen. I had always heard that the Folies Bergères was very immoral, and there was a pretty good chance that I should be grabbed up by one of those French *cocottes* and dragged off to some hell-hole, willy *and* nilly. I might not have made much of a hit with the *demi-monde* in my own country, but I saw no way out of a complete collapse of my moral fibre now. I even dashed a bit of cologne on my lapel.

After I got back from the Folies Bergères I read a copy of *Collier's* that I had bought on a newsstand and had a really good night's sleep. There was a corking good story in *Collier's* about a man who owned a sheep-dog that barked when the house caught fire. I shall never forget it.

Day followed day in Paris, a typically French trick. In my desire to see life I went to the Louvre, but it was closed on account of the theft of the Mona Lisa, which had occurred just that week. I went to Napoleon's Tomb, but there was nothing doing there. It was *la grande semaine* in Paris, and the chestnut trees were all dying off. *Zut alors!*

* * * * *

My nights were spent in looking for adventure, which I found in various forms. A place called Mitchell's, on Montmartre, served wheatcakes and sausages just like those in New York, and over on the Left Bank, the home of the Bohemians, I found a man from Worcester who was studying book-binding and wanted to know all about the home folks. He introduced me to a drink which was something like iced tea without the kick. The ham sandwiches were also pretty bad.

July 1 in Paris! Would wonders never cease? Would I ever get back to New York?

THE END